CW01666132

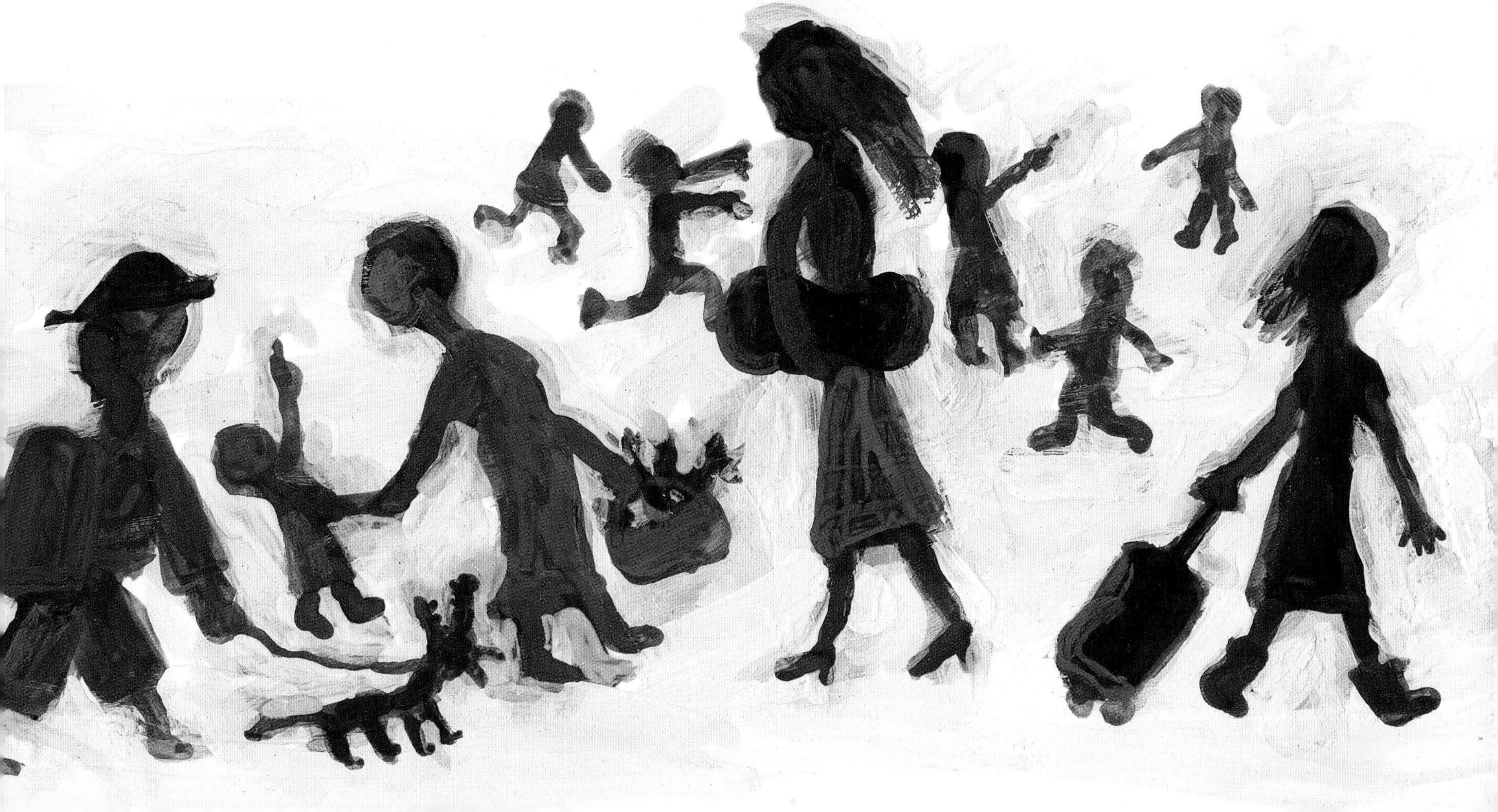

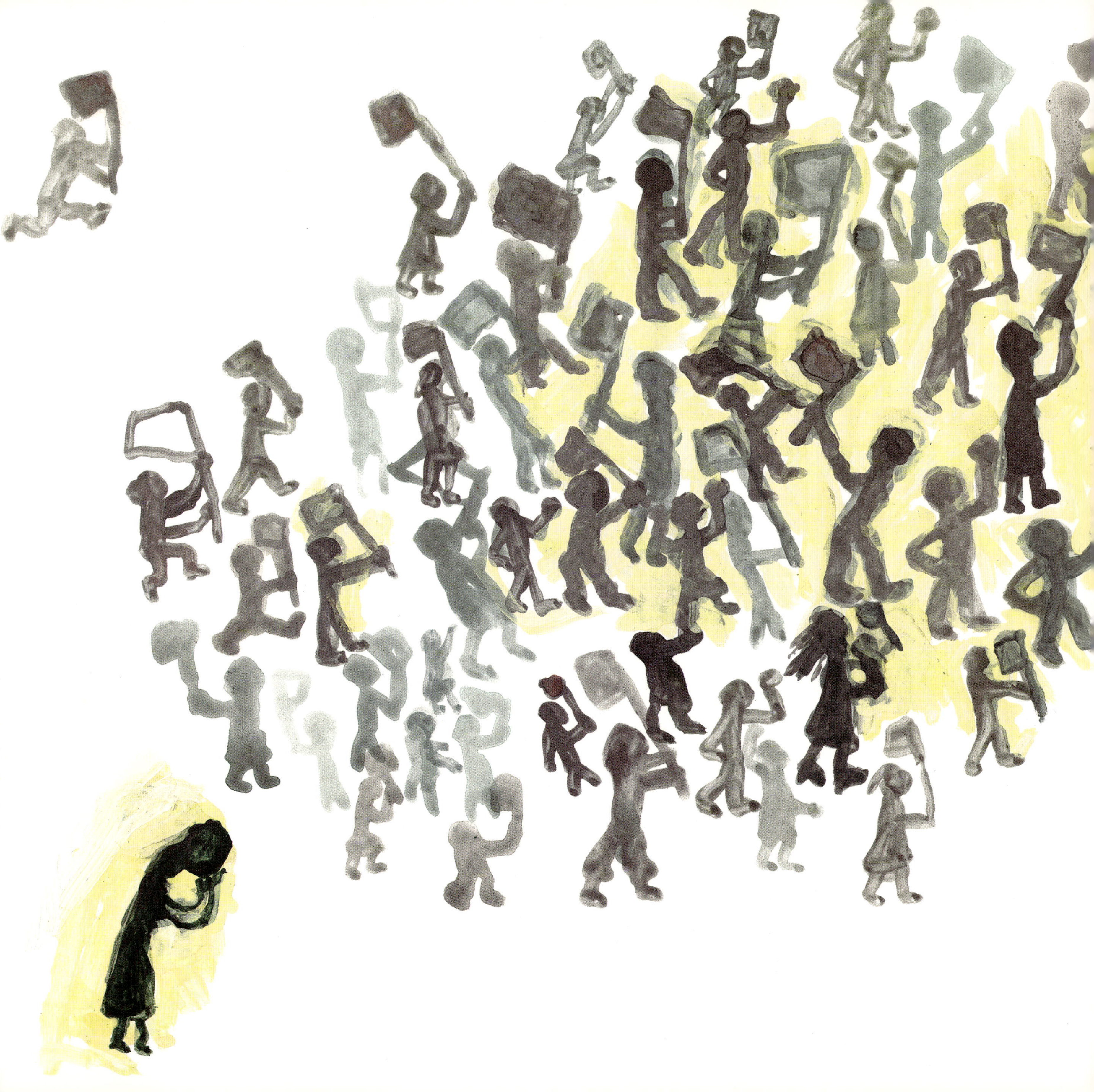

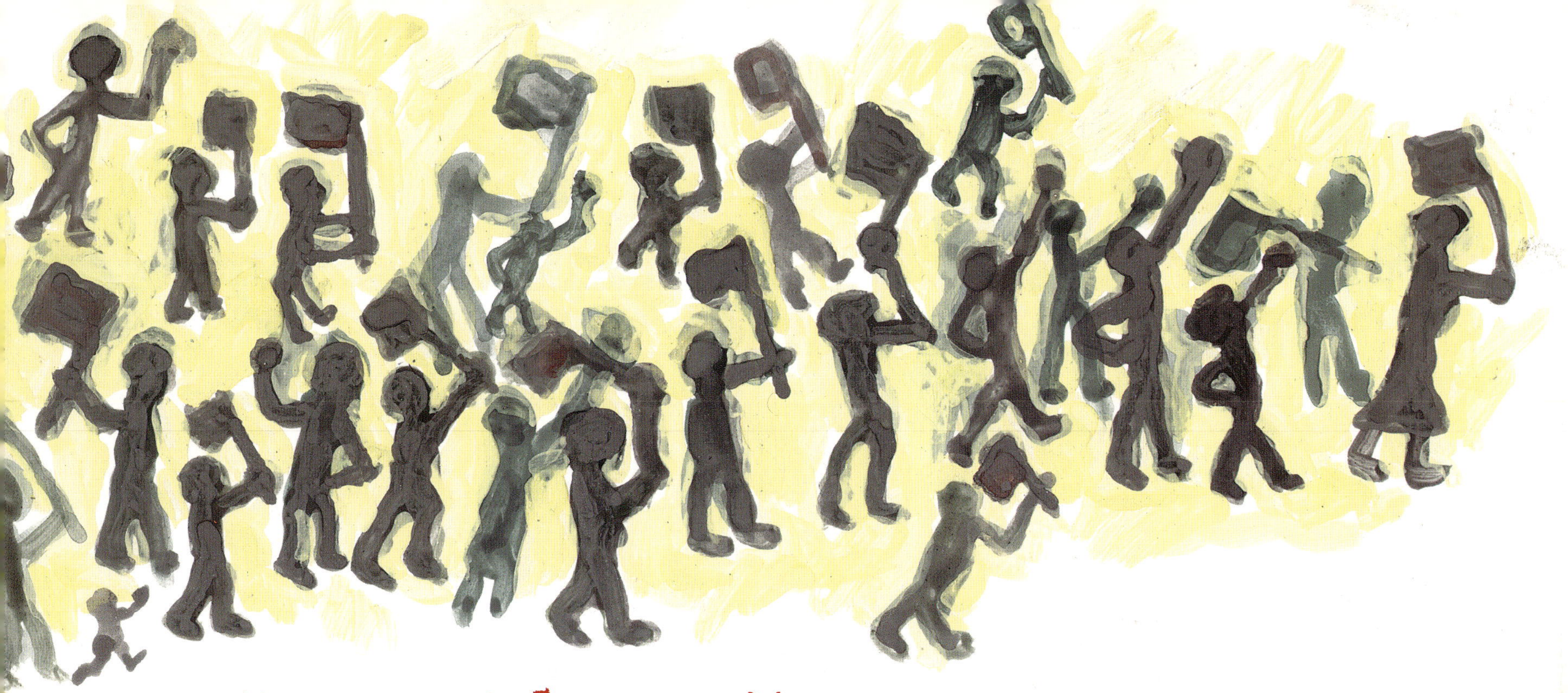

Can You Hear My Voice?

Written and Illustrated by Seizo Tashima
Translated by Michael Hughes

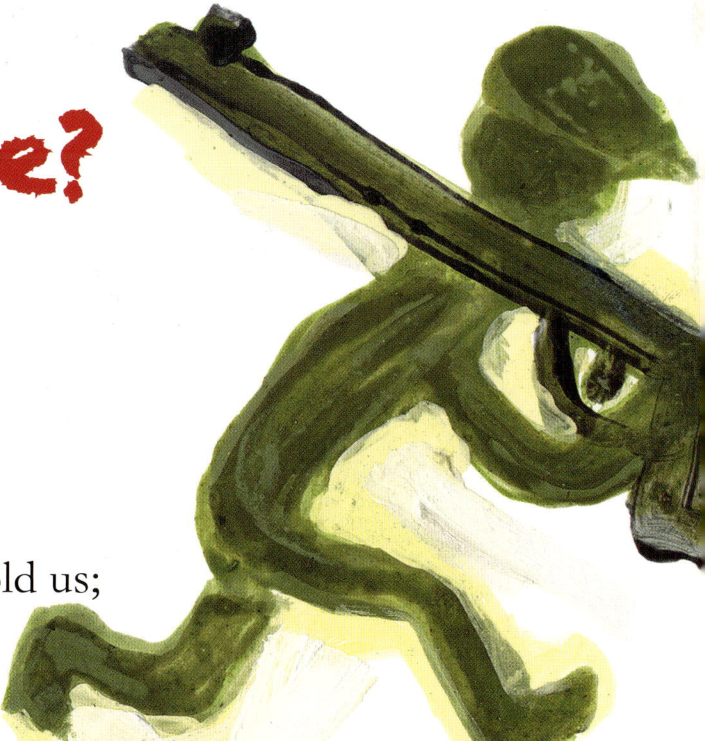

"*Fight for your country!*" they told us;
and off I went to war.

Only my mama was crying. "*Goodbye mama!*"

XANADU

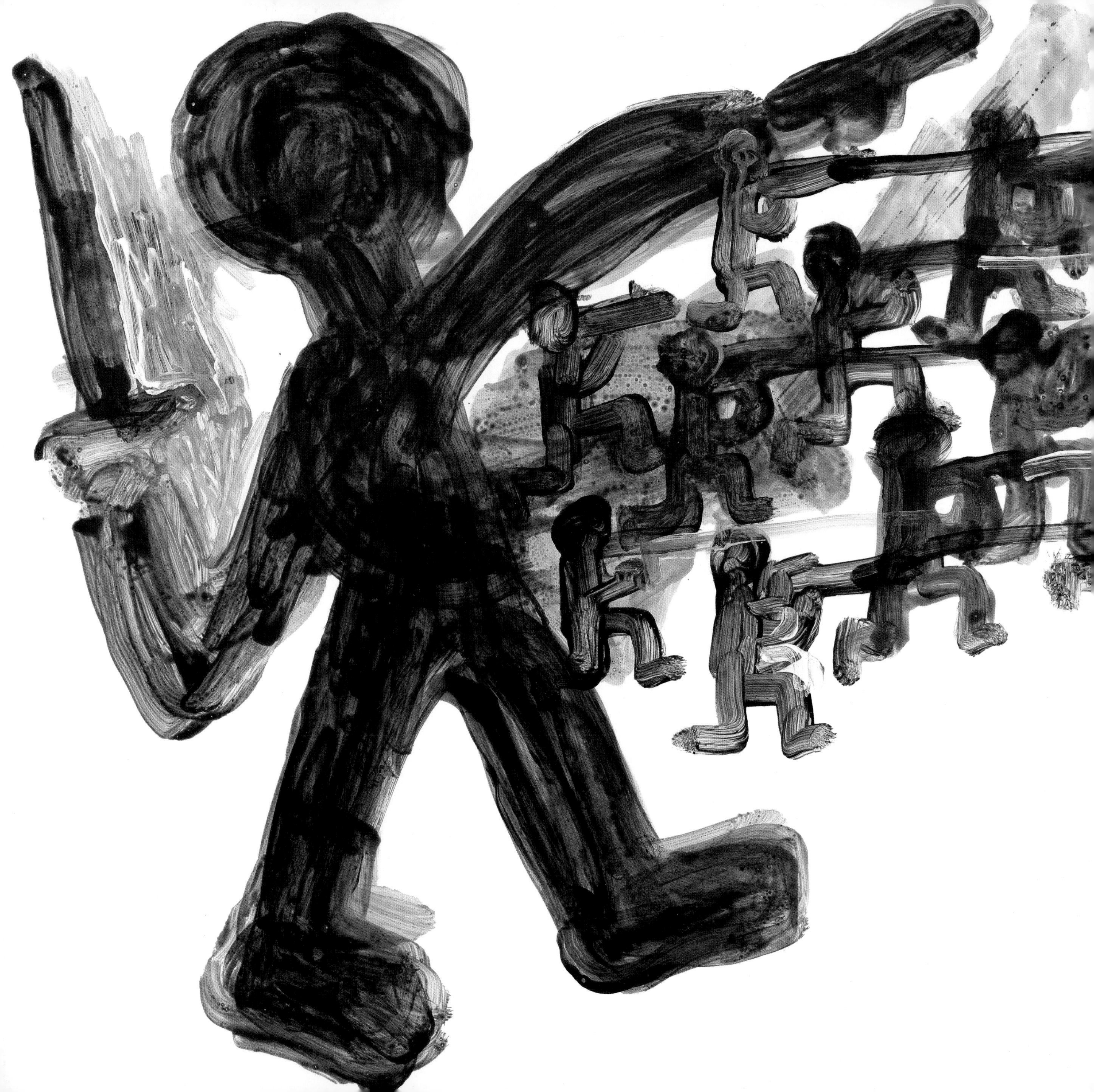

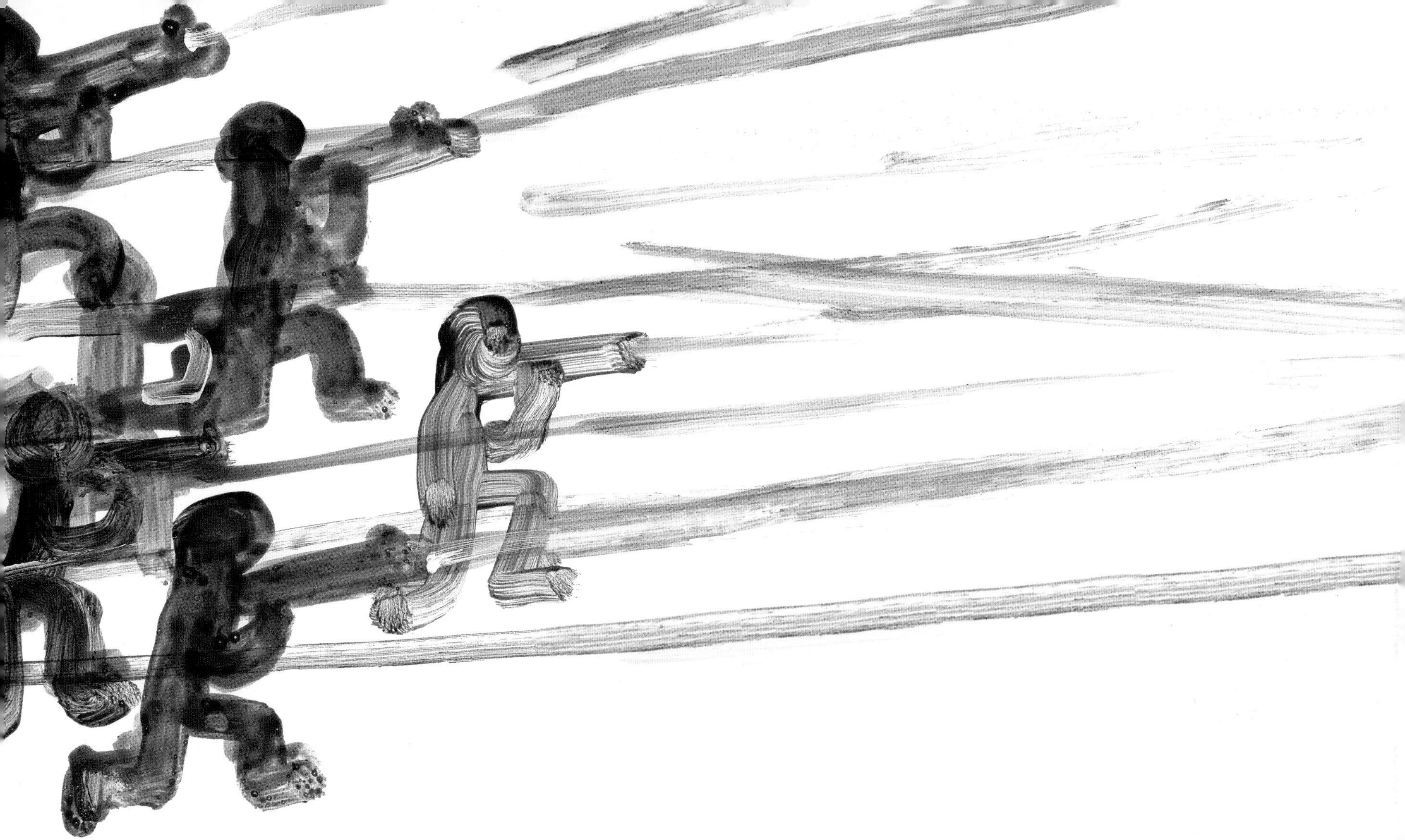

I had my orders. So I shot my gun.
At fellow human beings.

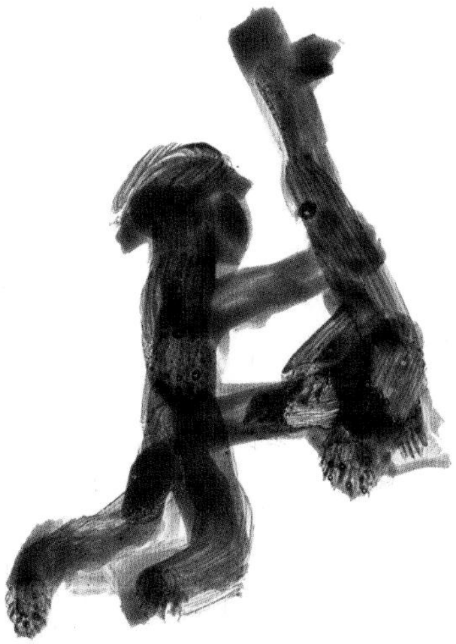

The enemy's shells came flying towards me. There was nowhere to run, nowhere to hide.

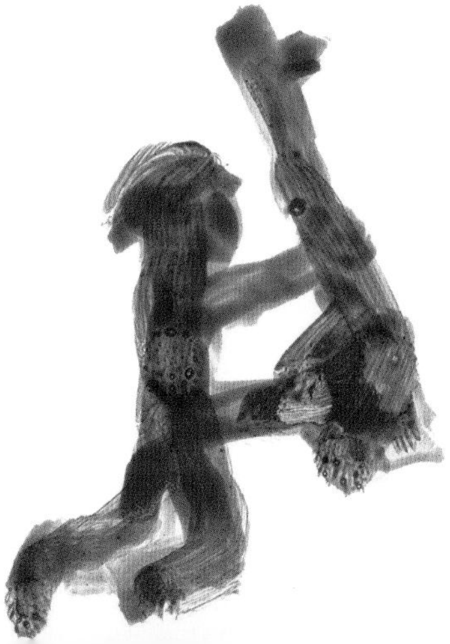

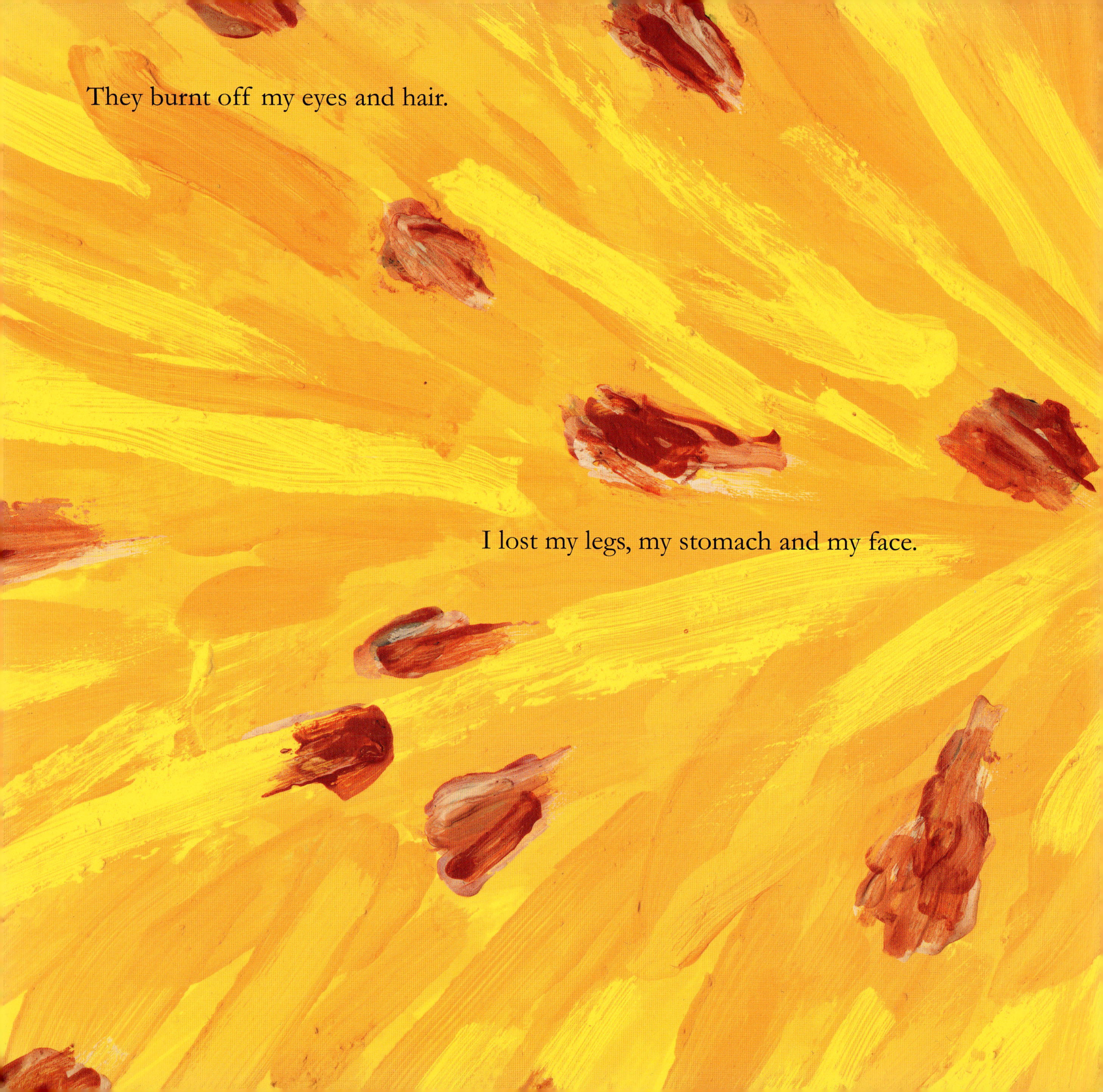

They burnt off my eyes and hair.

I lost my legs, my stomach and my face.

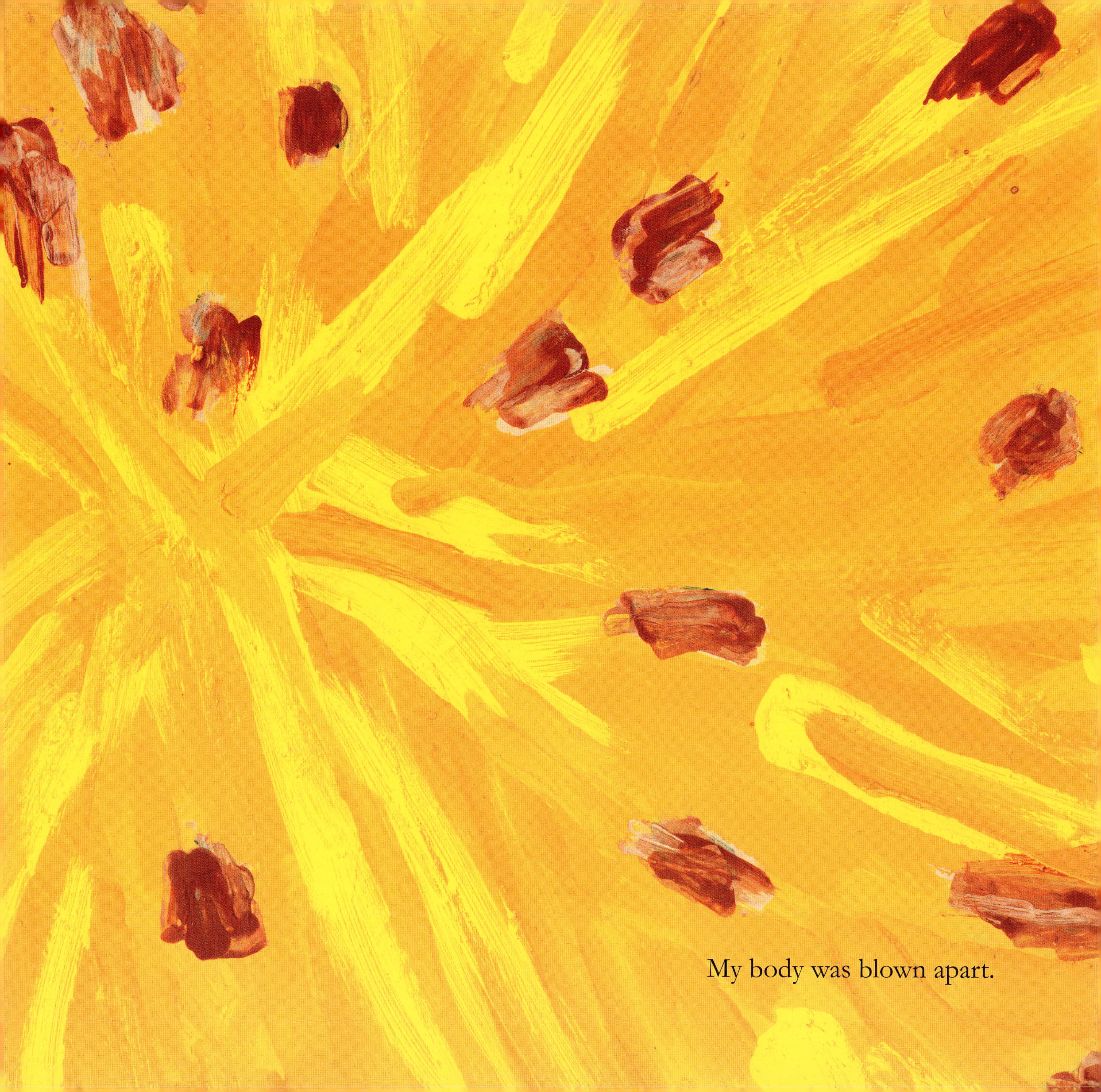

My body was blown apart.

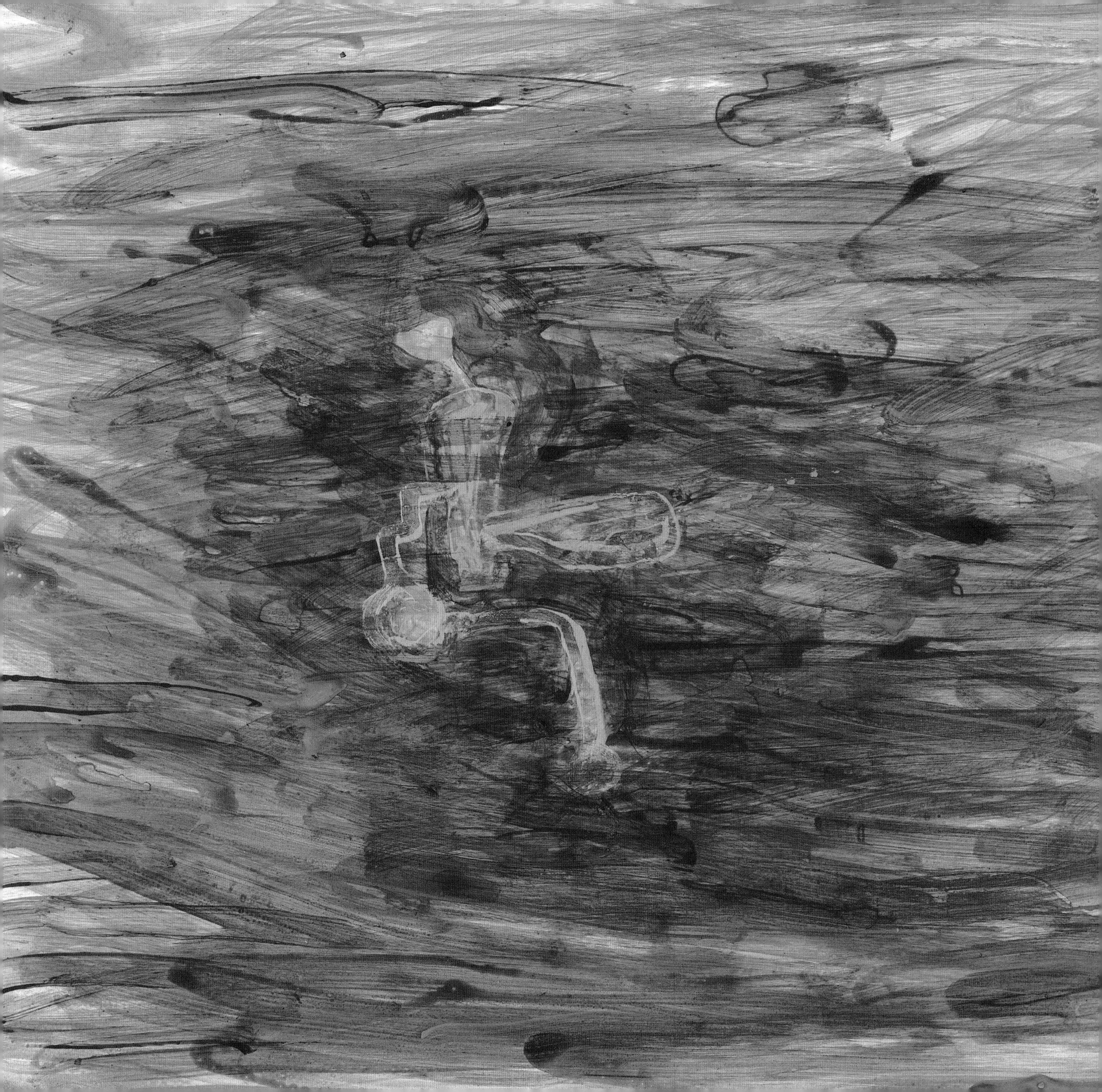

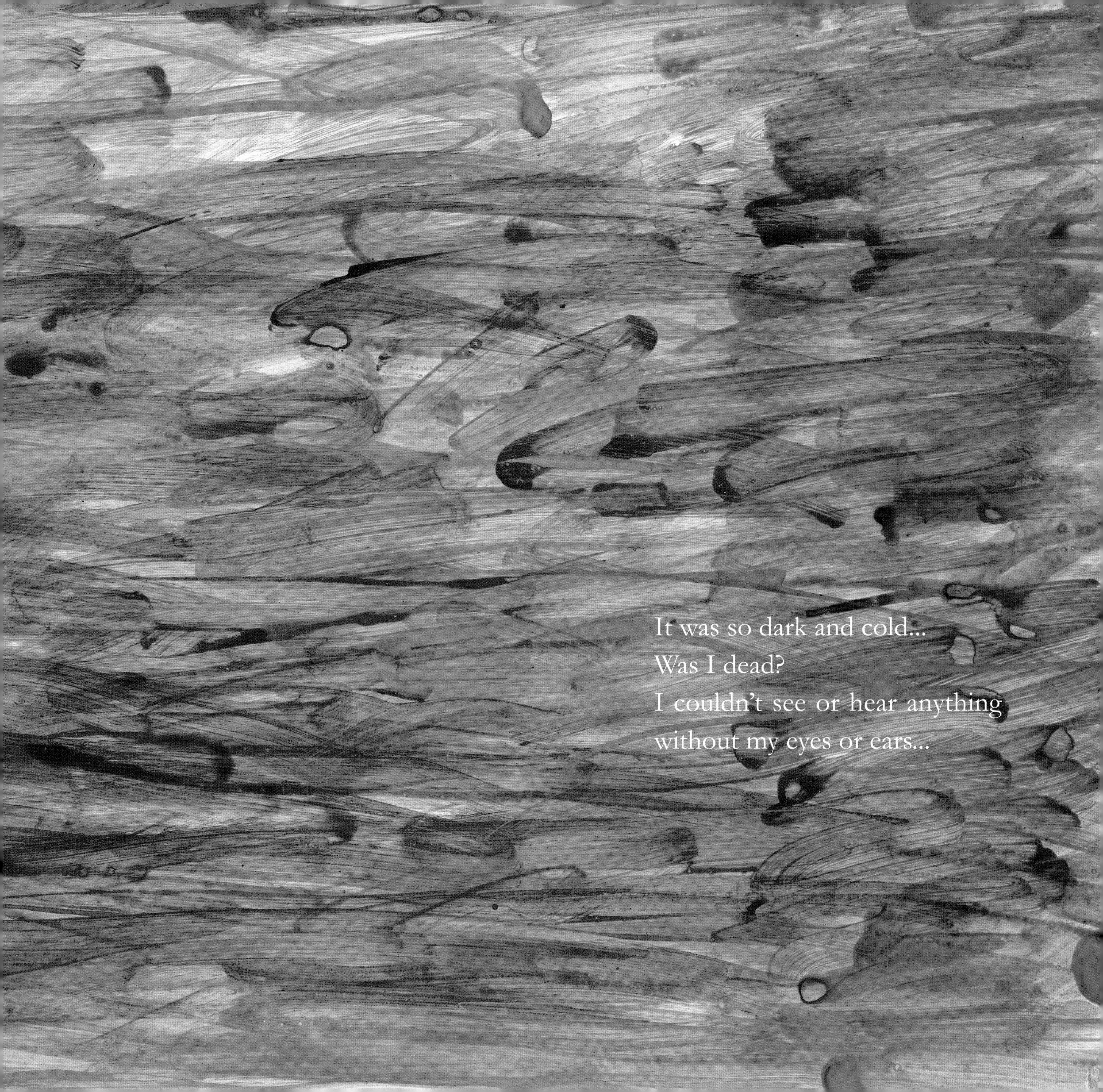

It was so dark and cold...
Was I dead?
I couldn't see or hear anything
without my eyes or ears...

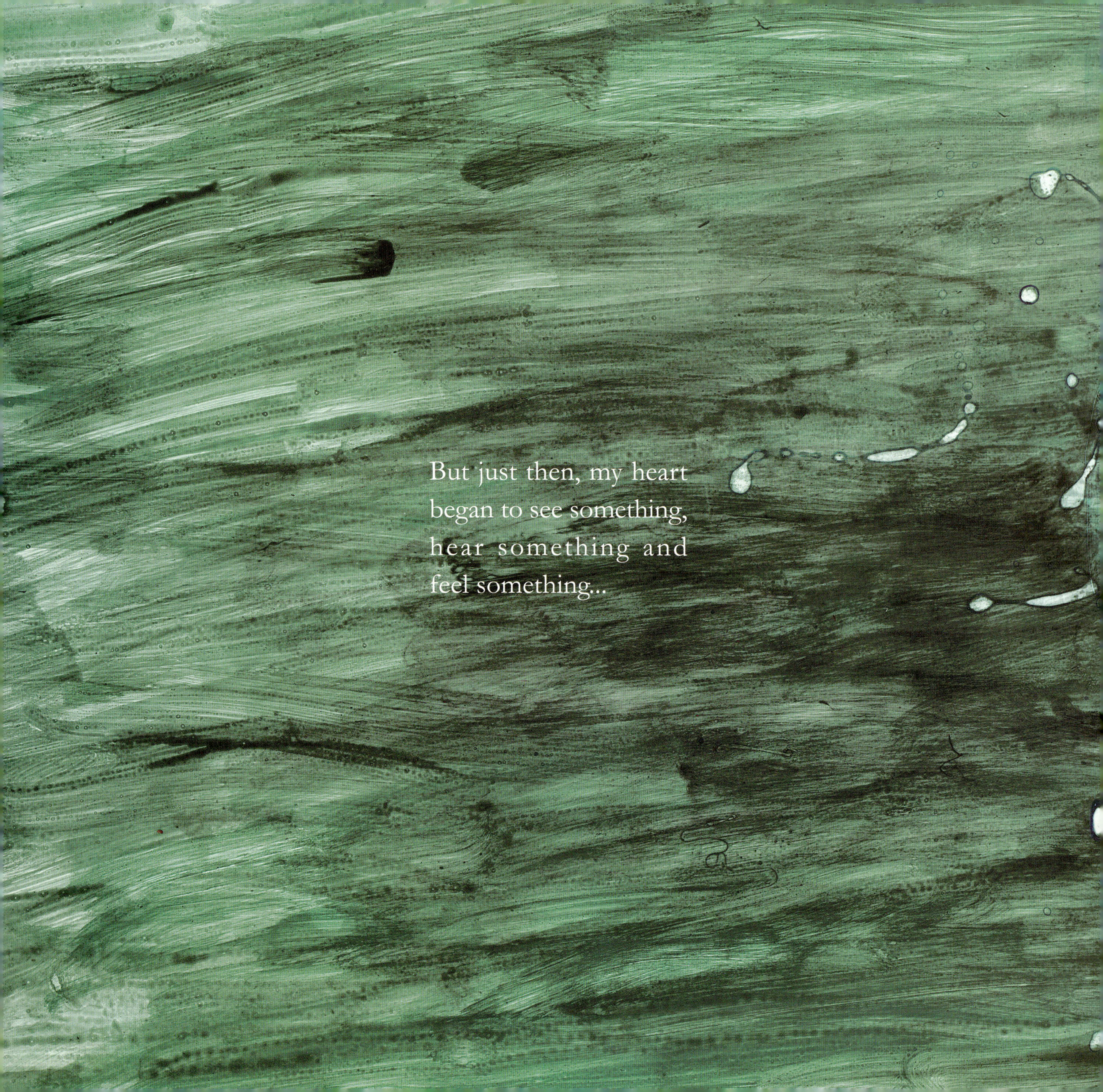

But just then, my heart began to see something, hear something and feel something...

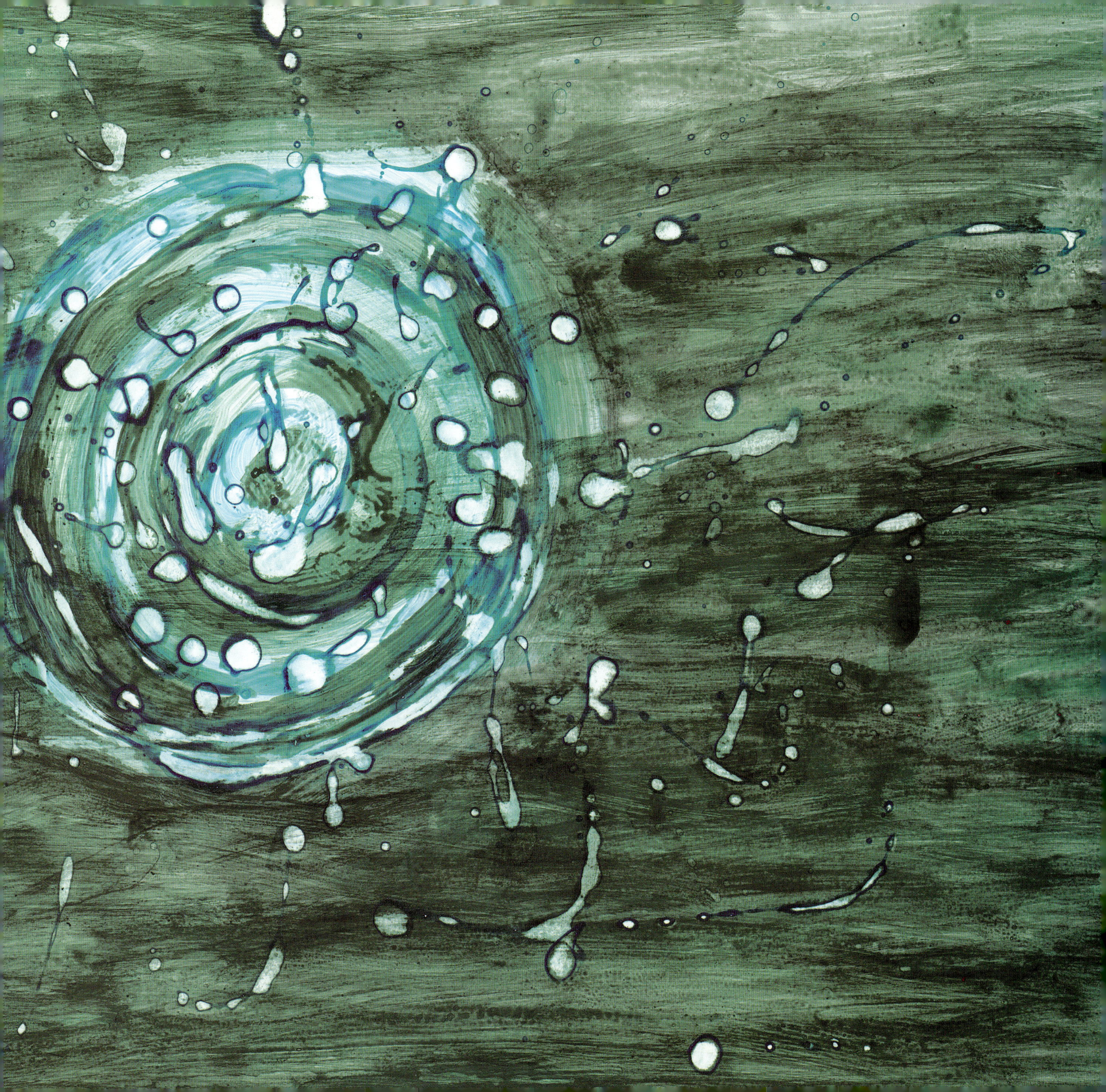

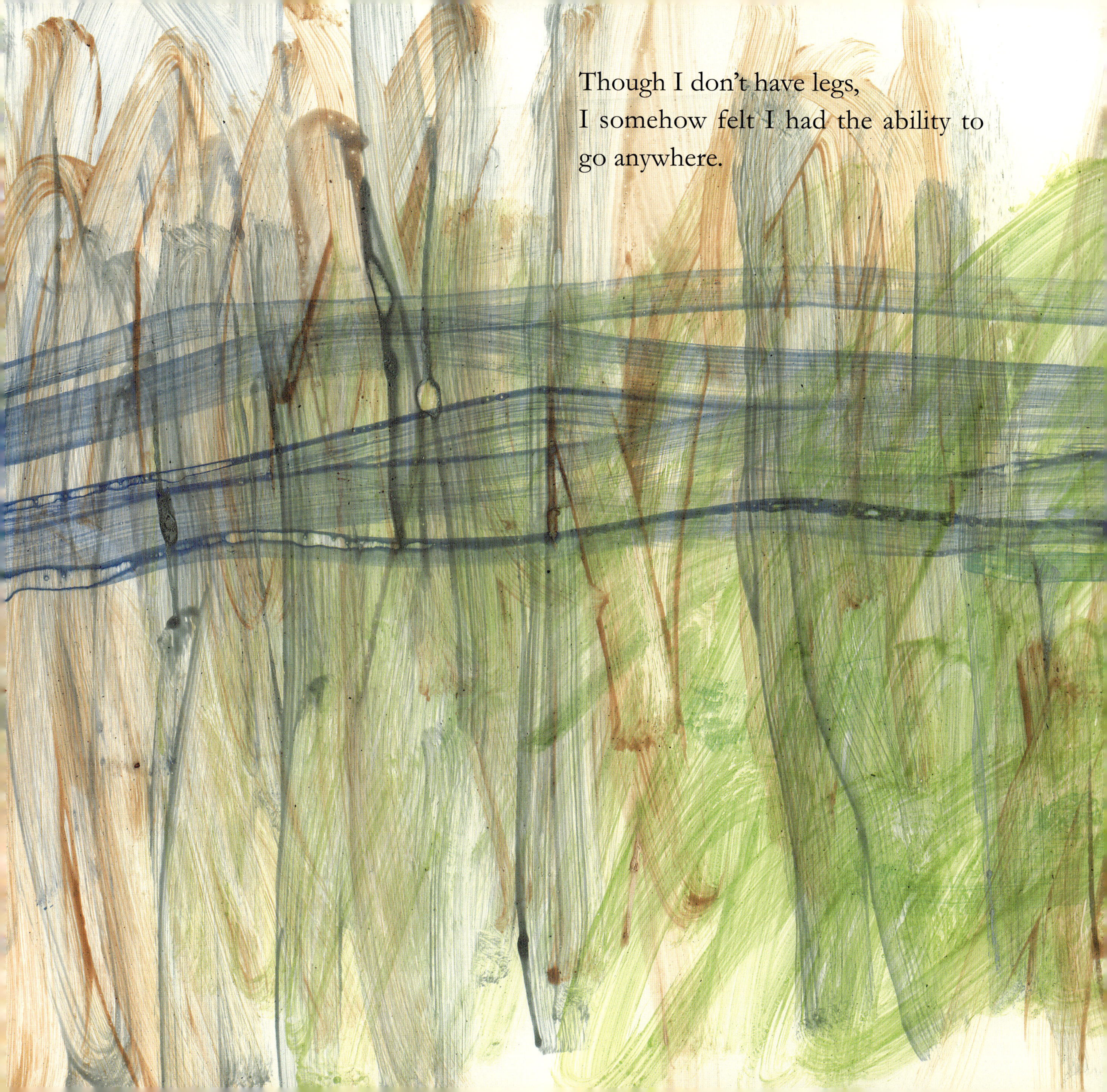

Though I don't have legs,
I somehow felt I had the ability to
go anywhere.

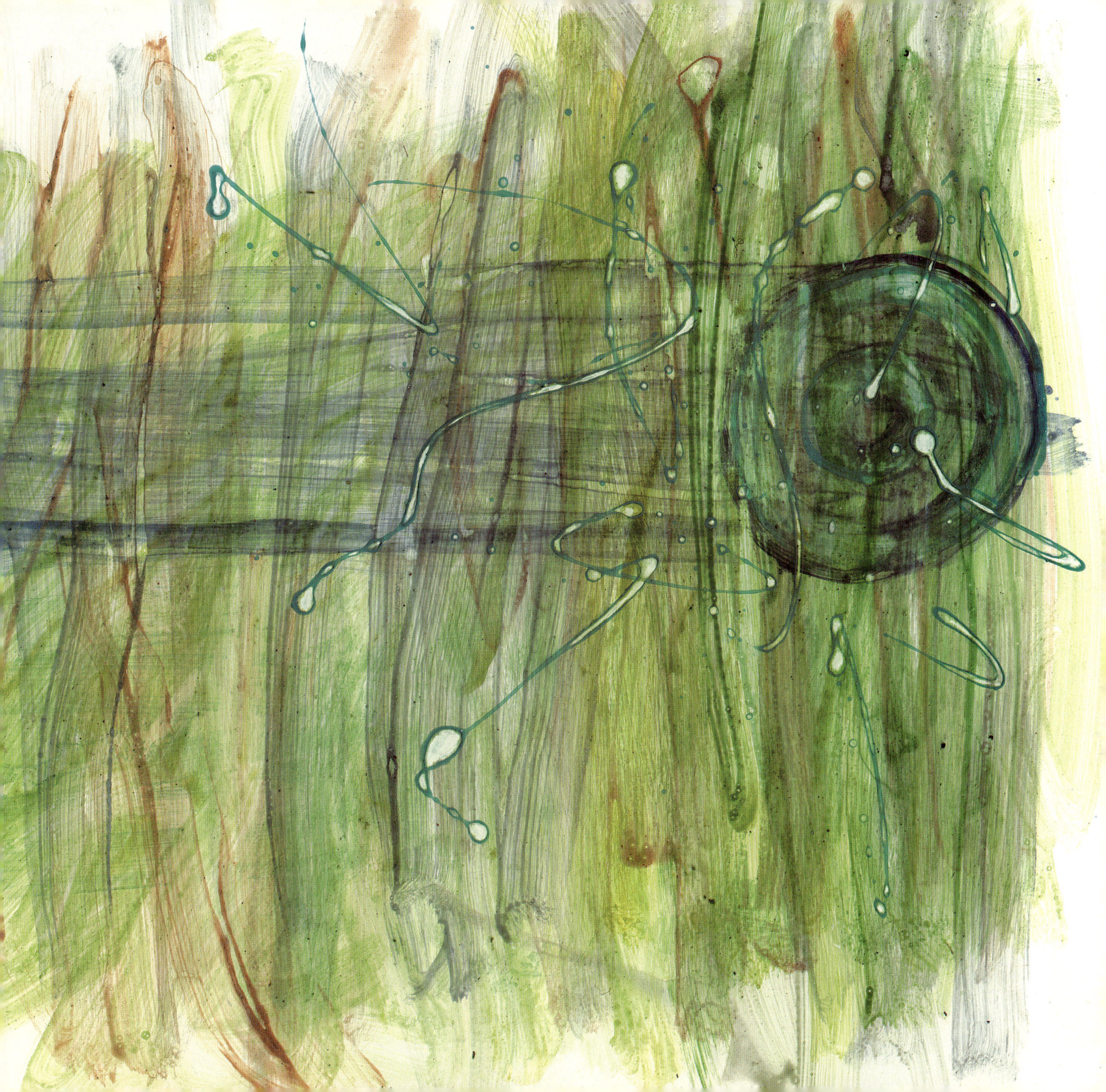

My mama was crying.

Did she already know what had happened to me?

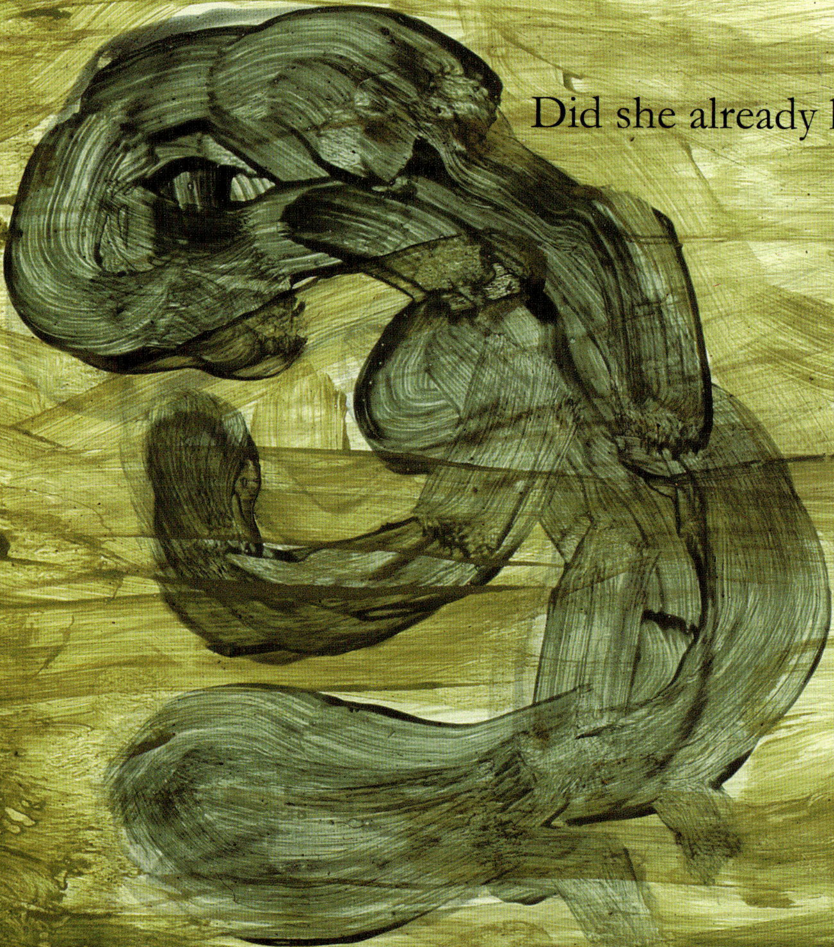

My little brother was red with anger.
“*I'll shoot the enemies for you!*” he said.

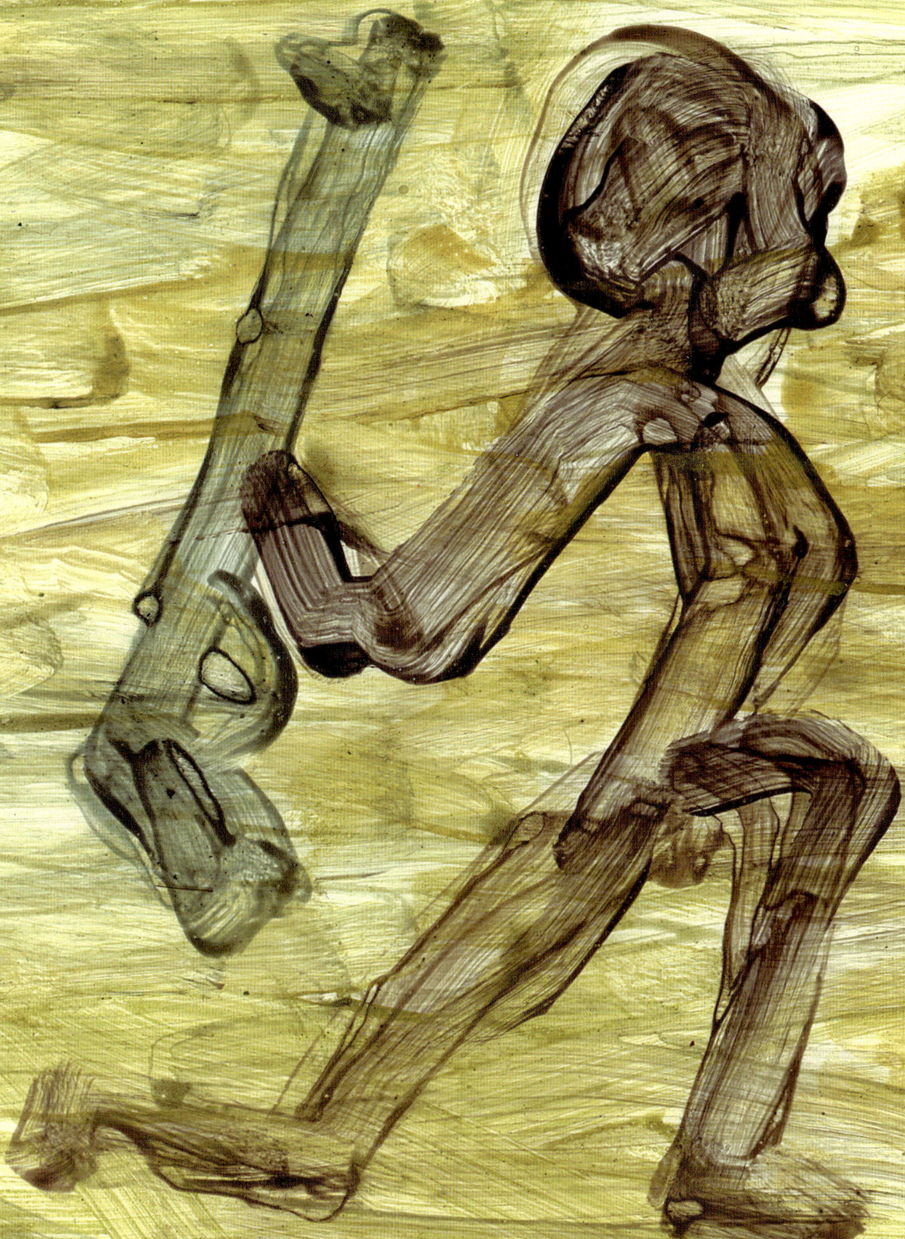

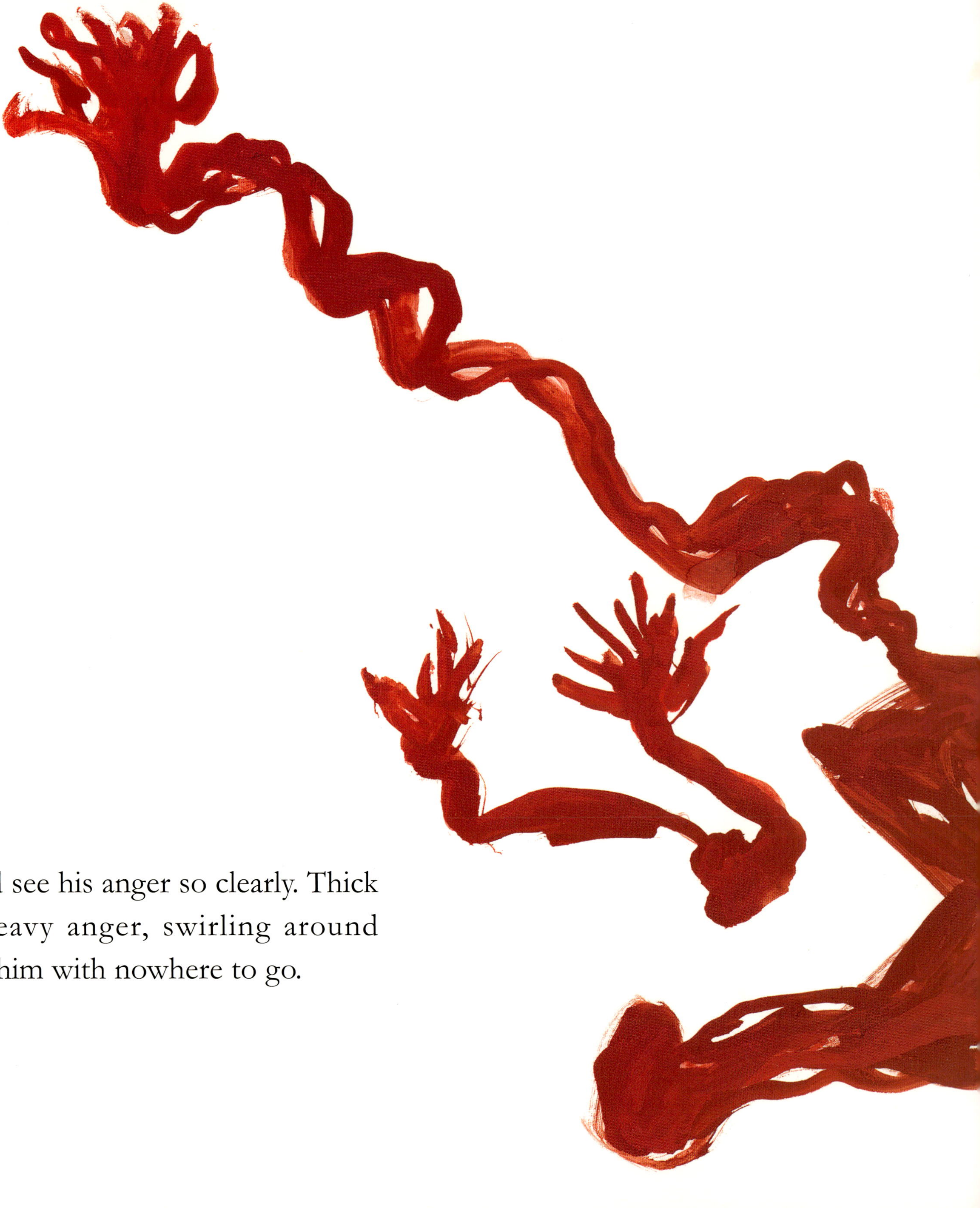

I could see his anger so clearly. Thick and heavy anger, swirling around inside him with nowhere to go.

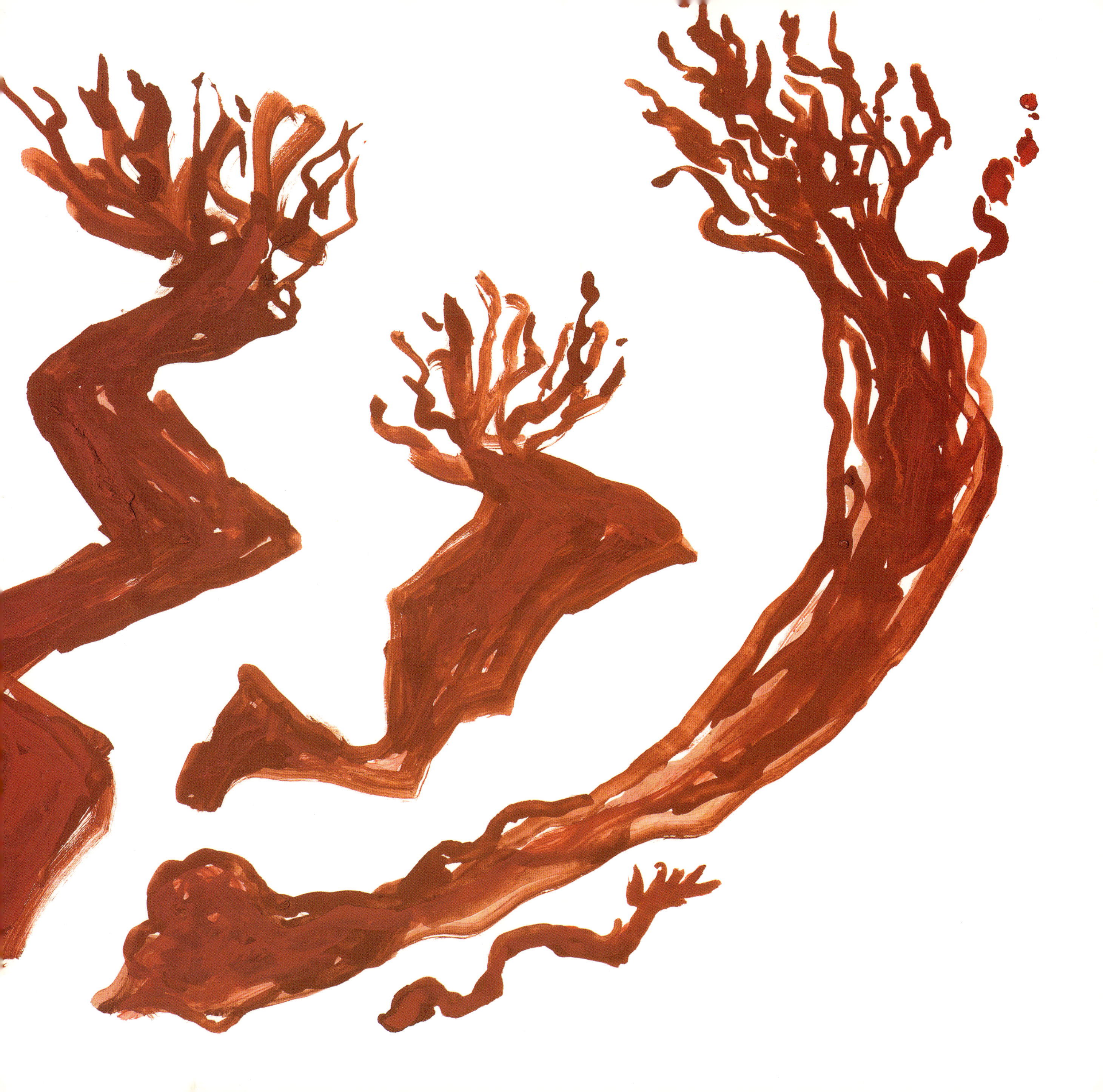

Oh no... was my little brother
heading to the battlefield too?

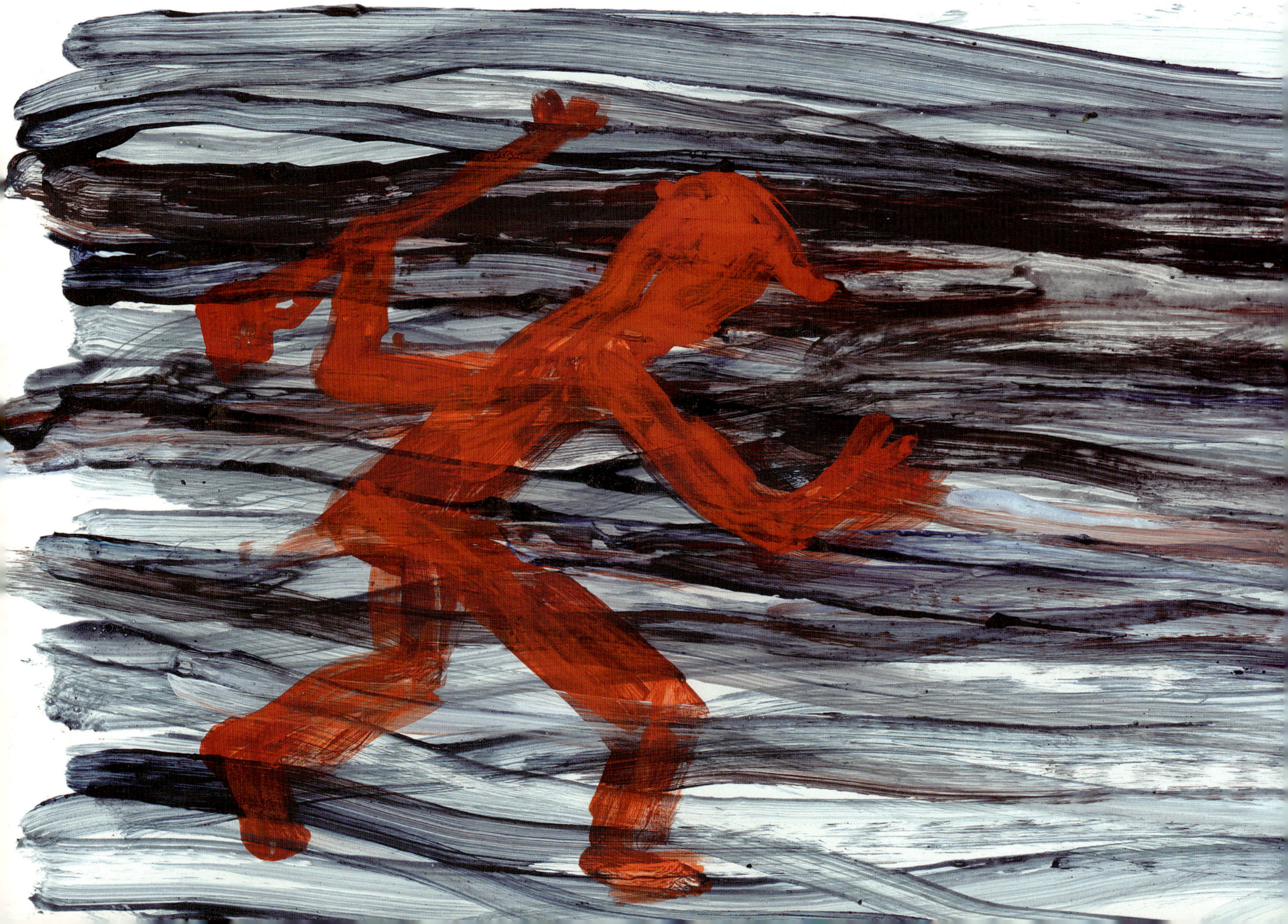

"*Don't!*" I yelled,
"*Mama will be left all by herself!*"

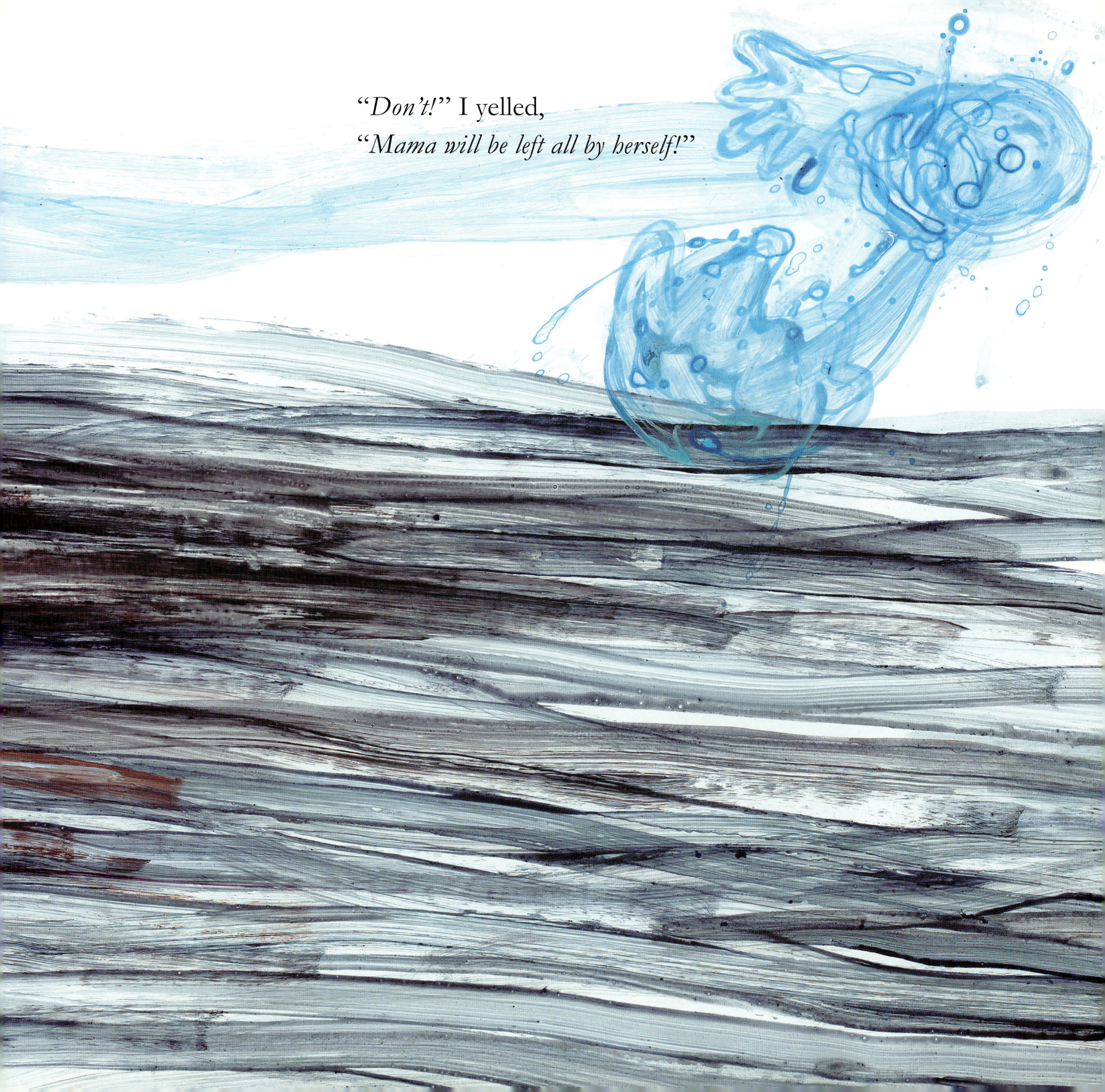

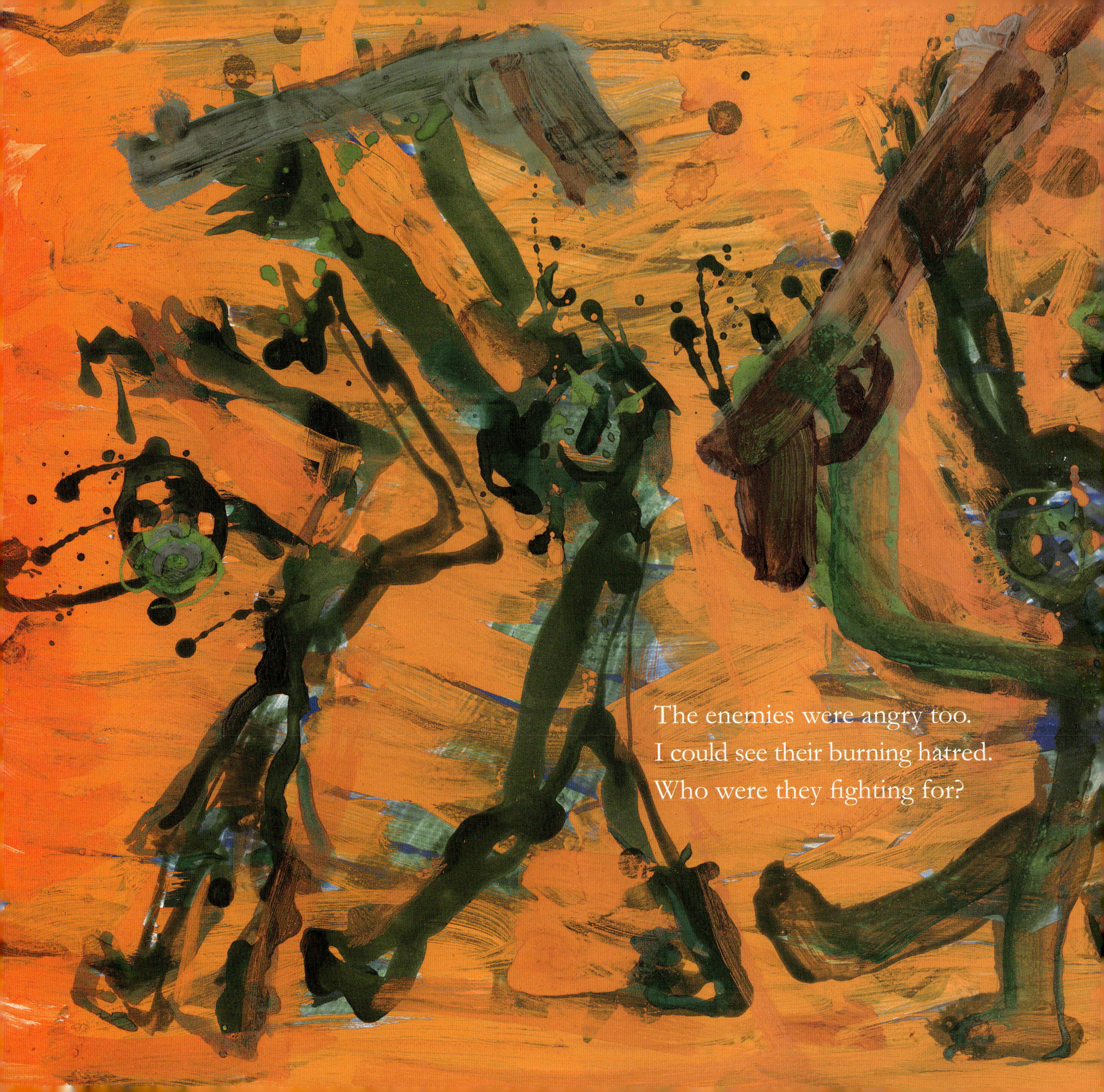

The enemies were angry too.
I could see their burning hatred.
Who were they fighting for?

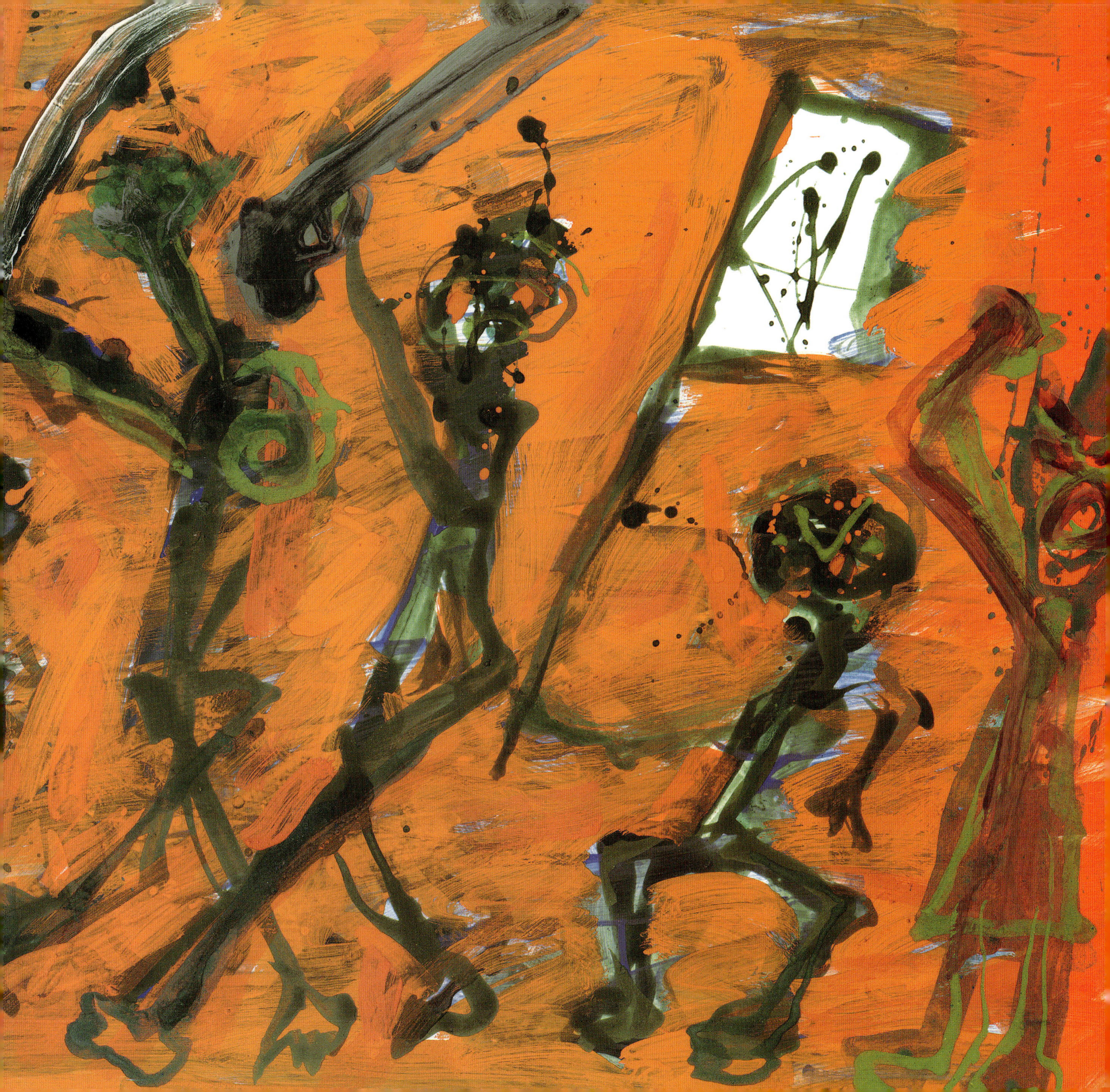

Who were we being killed for?

Who were we killing for?

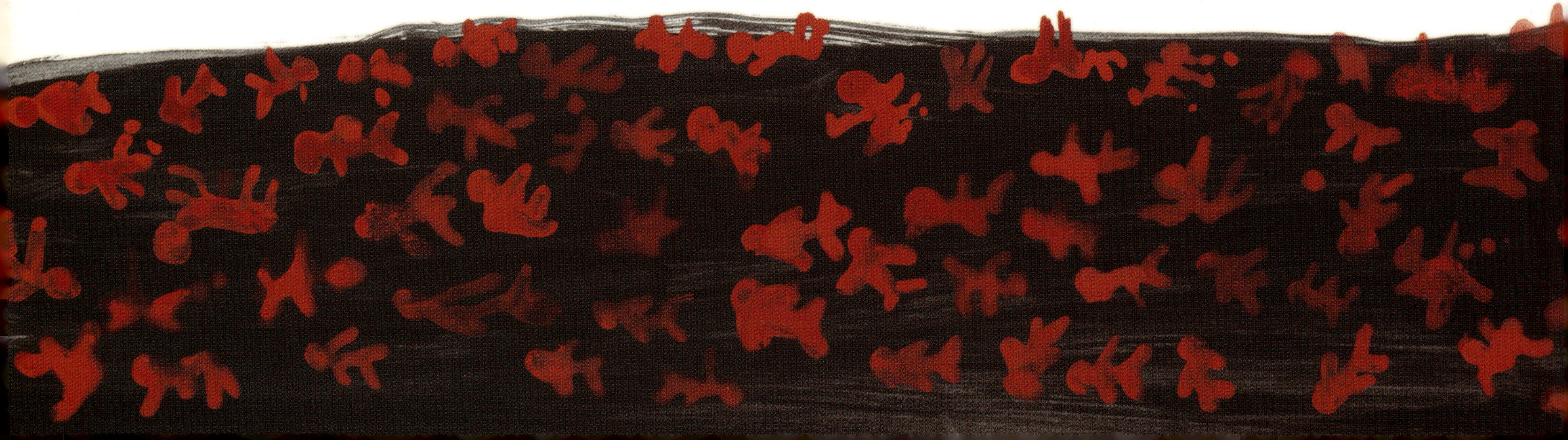

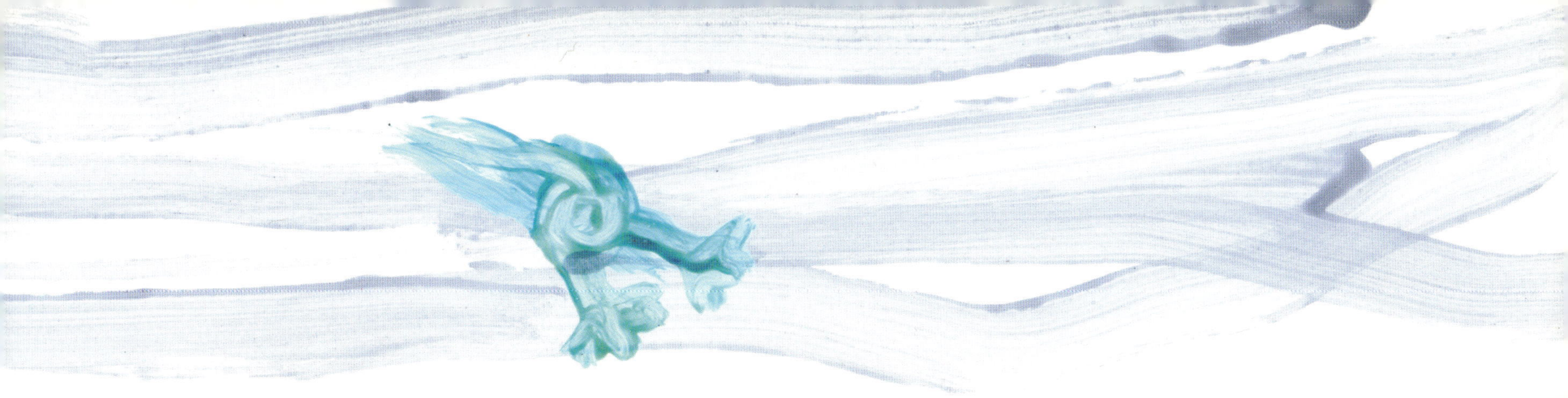

What were we dying for?

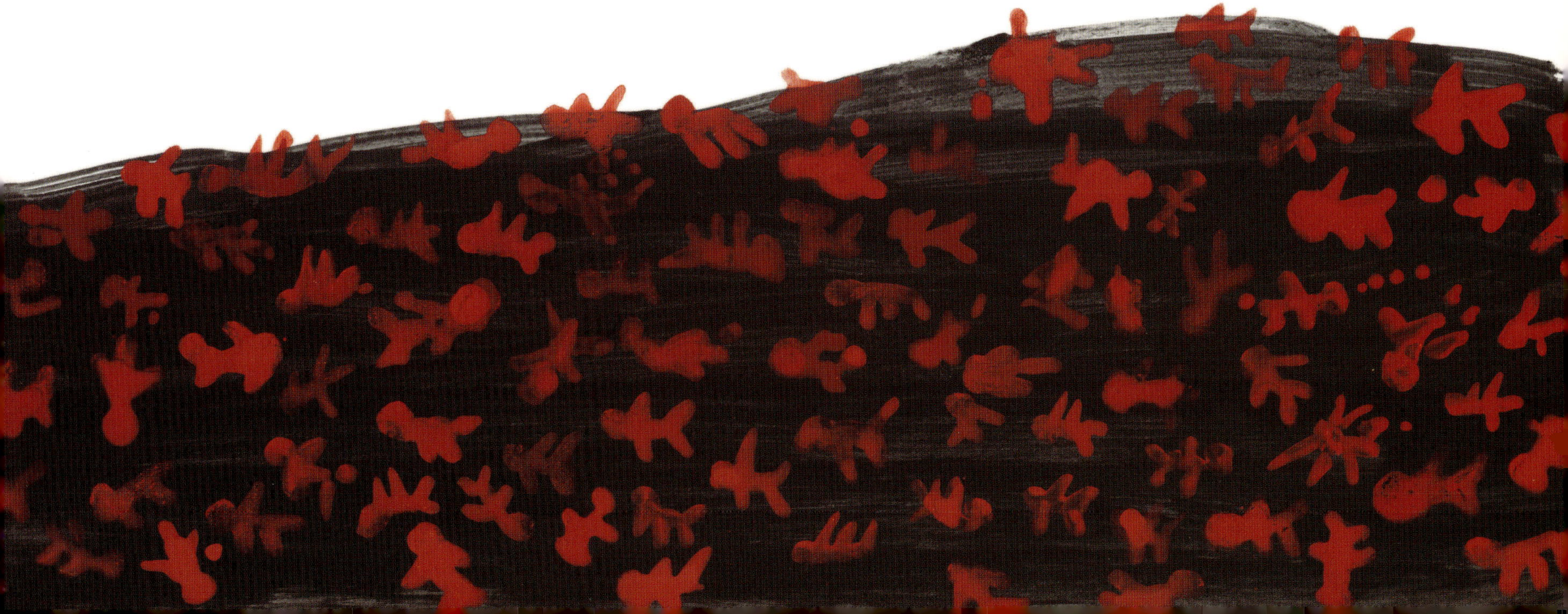

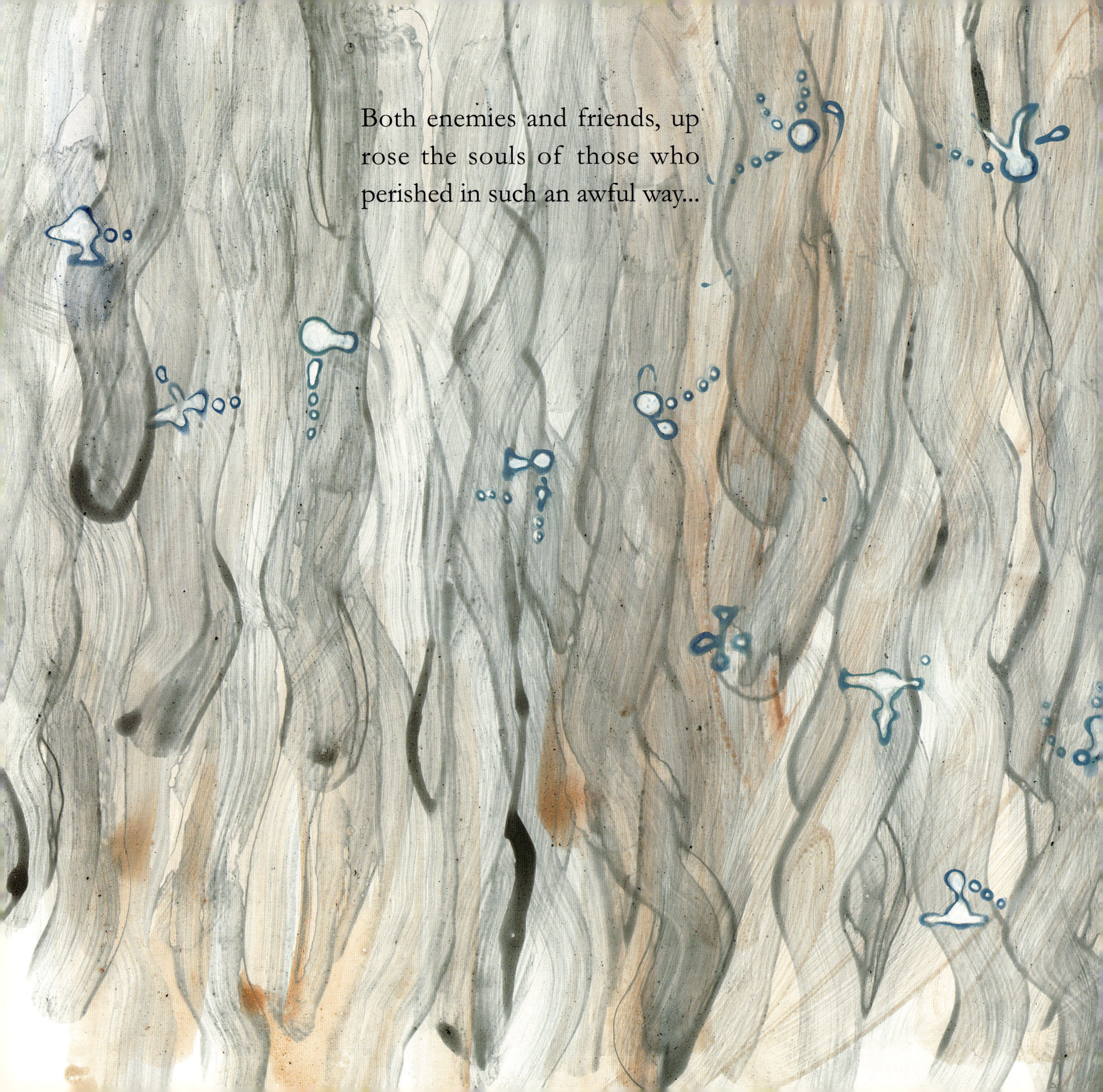

Both enemies and friends, up rose the souls of those who perished in such an awful way...

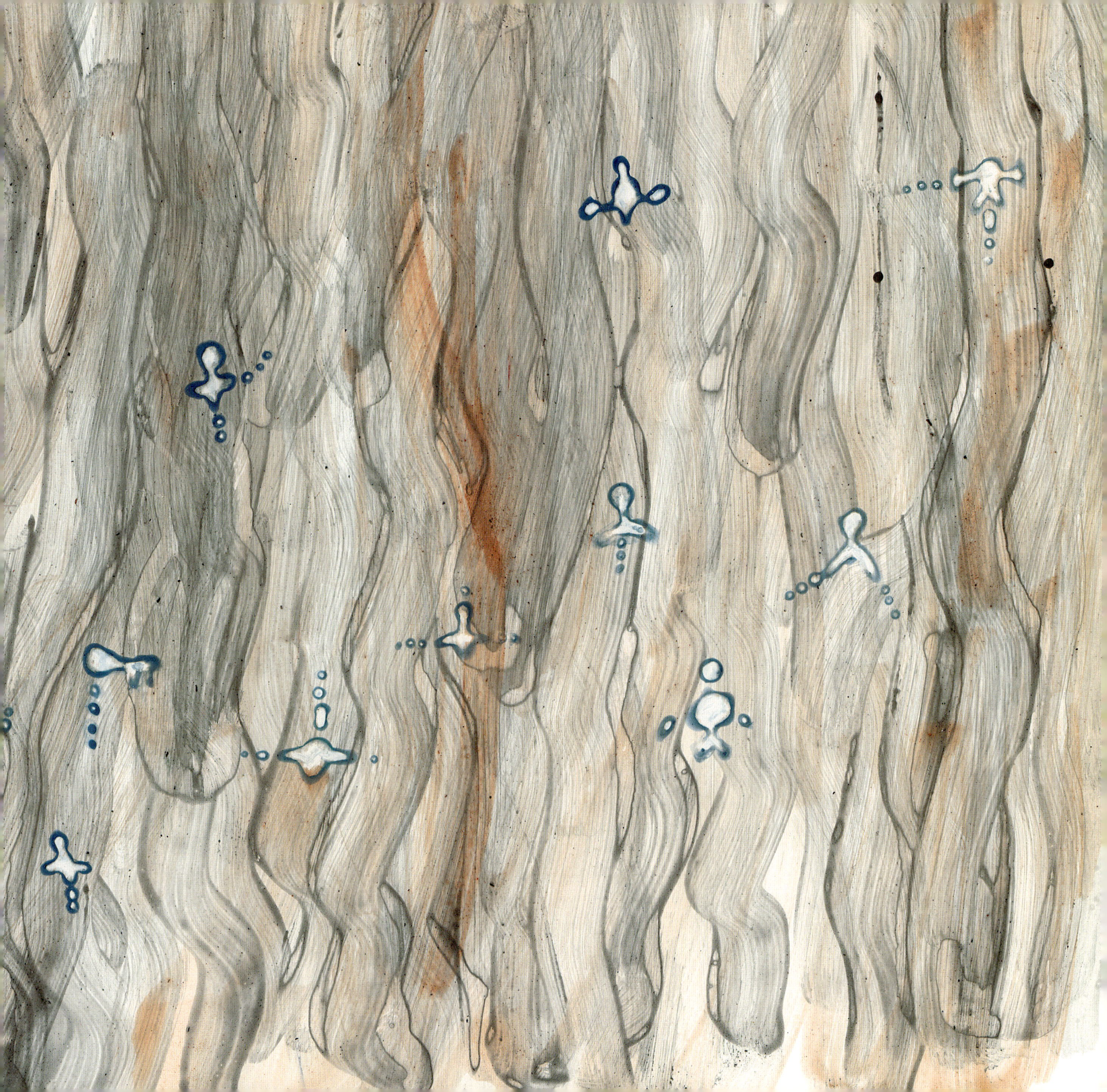

My little brother was dead.

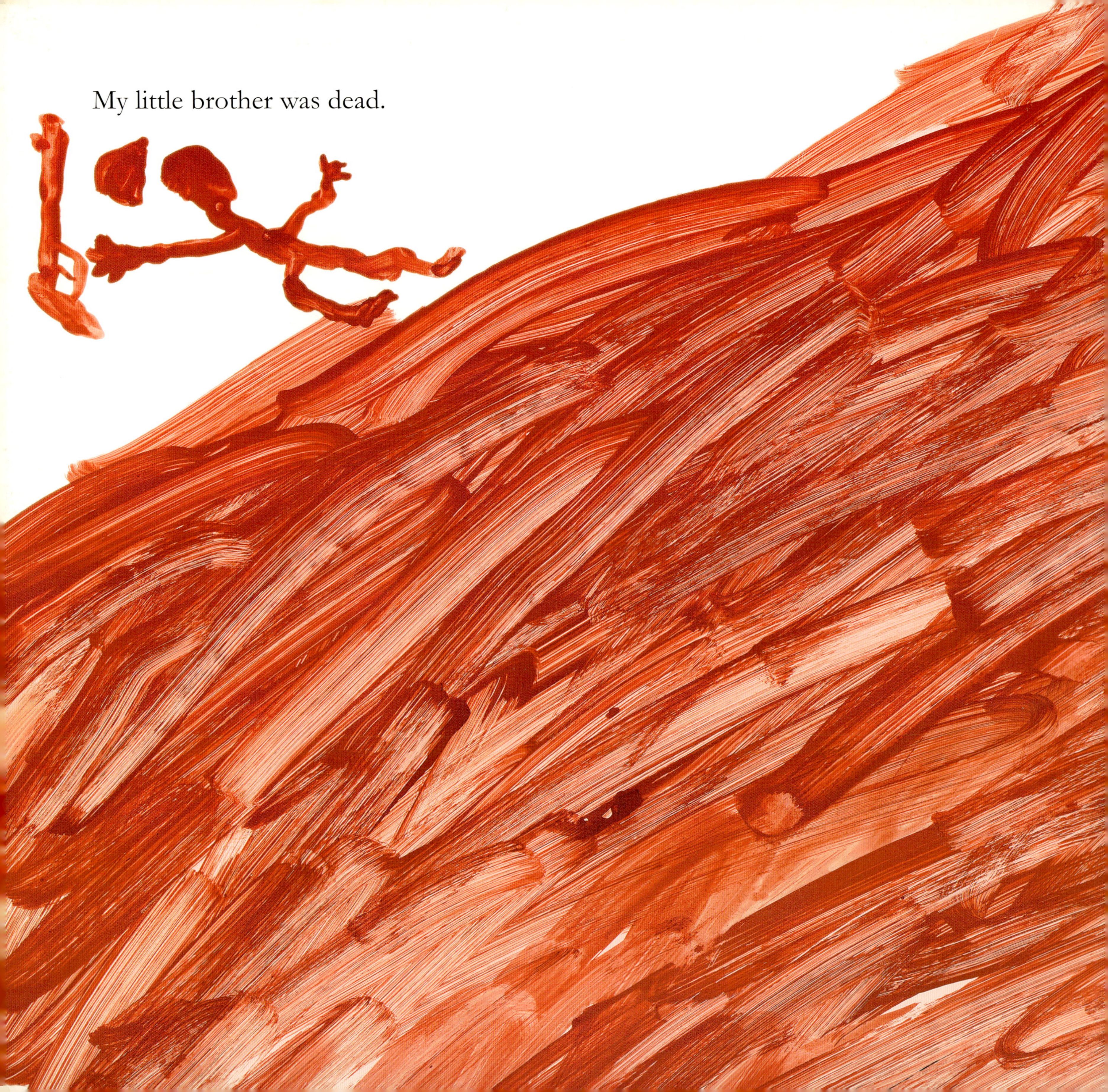

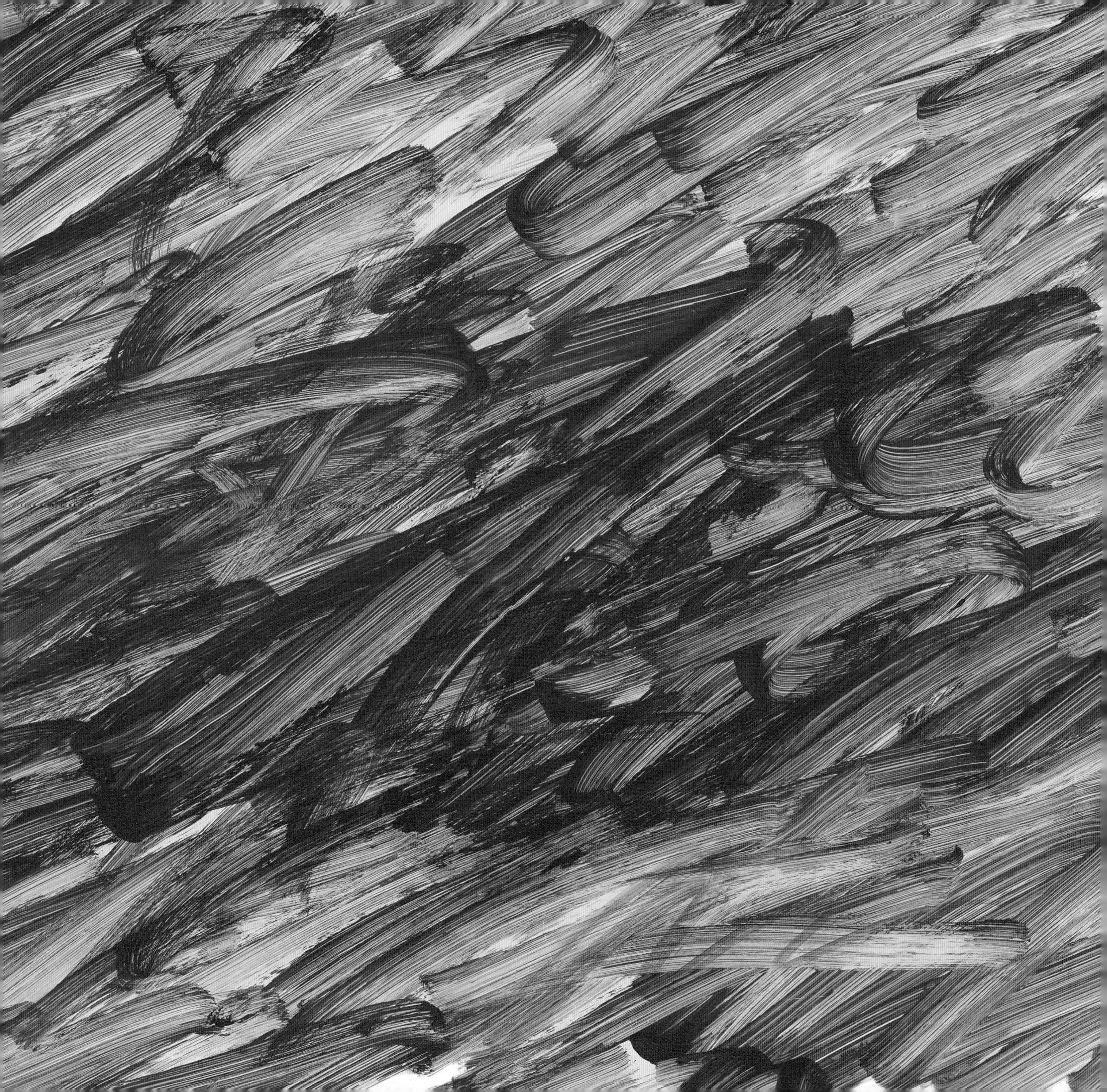

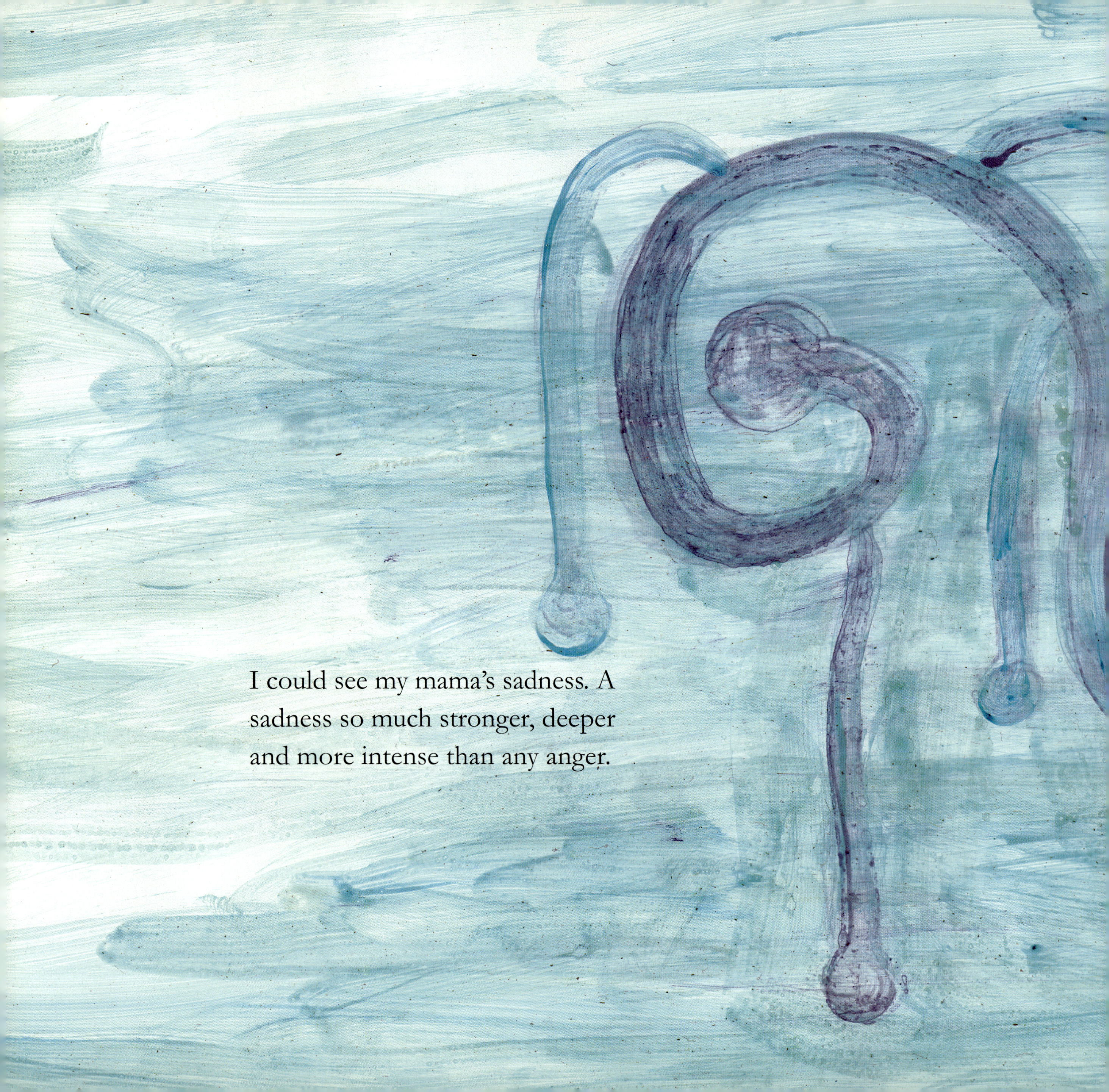

I could see my mama's sadness. A sadness so much stronger, deeper and more intense than any anger.

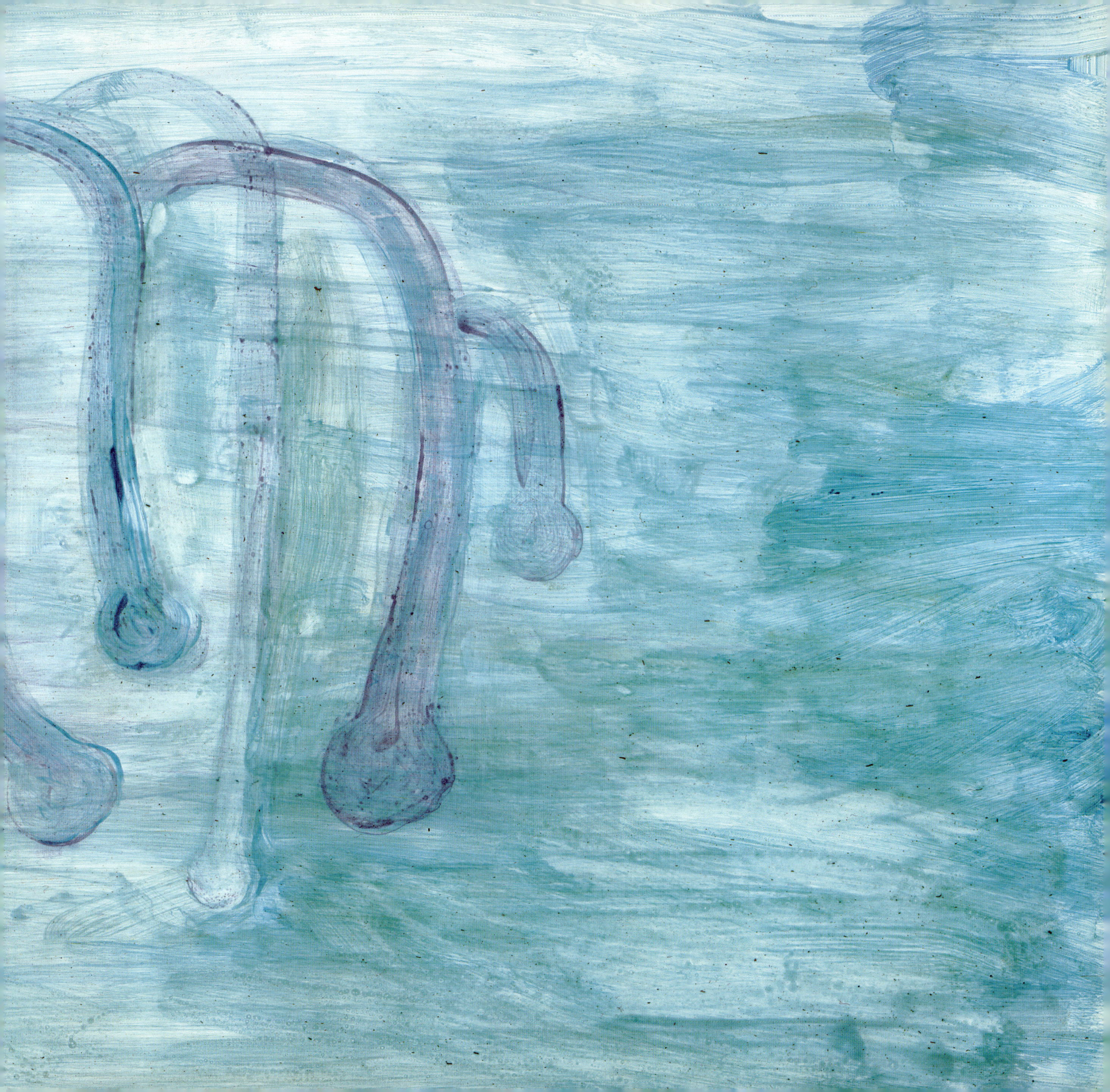

Even though no one can see me, I want to tell you about it...

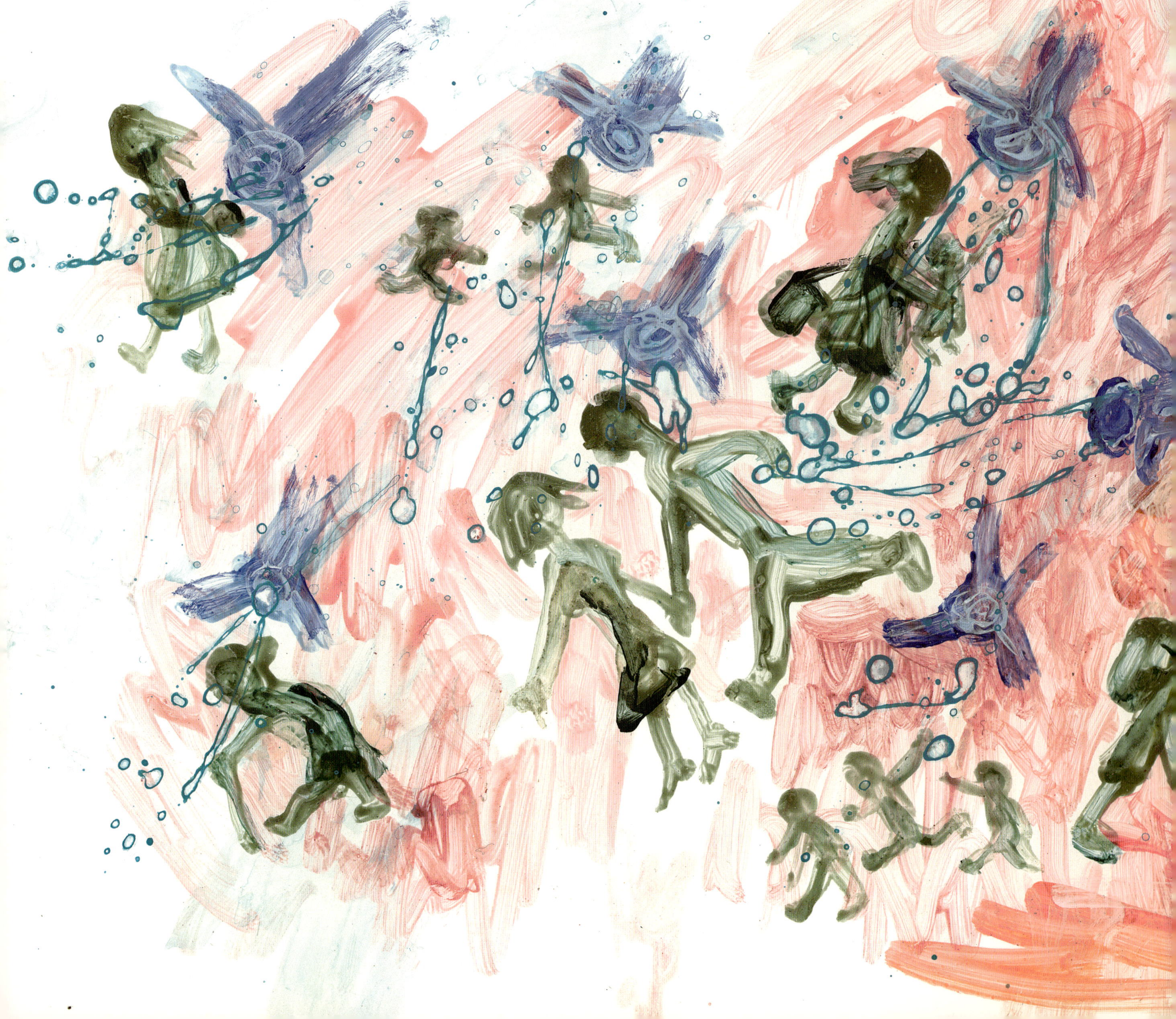

... about wars where people killed people; about people like us, who were once very much alive just like you.

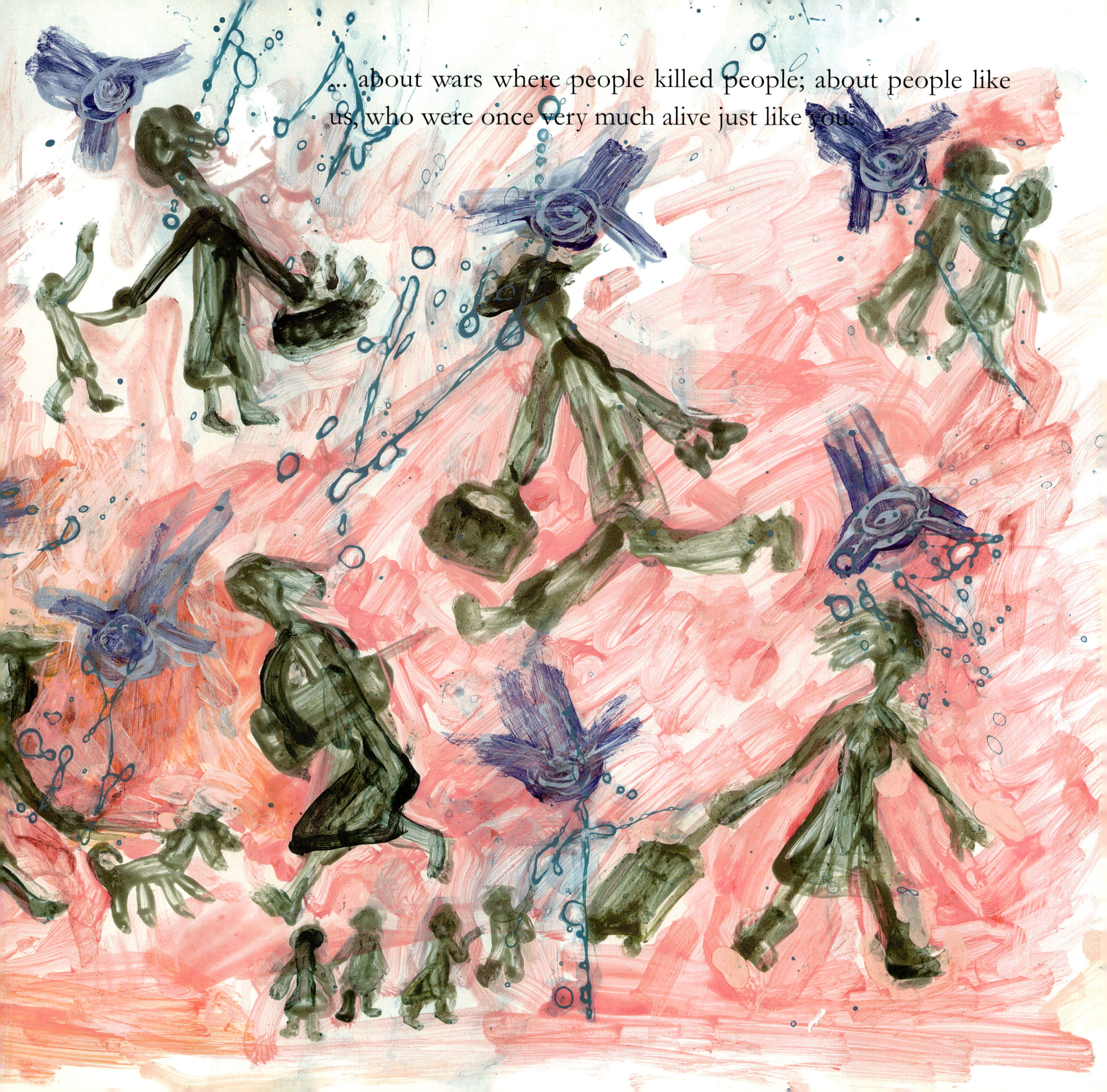

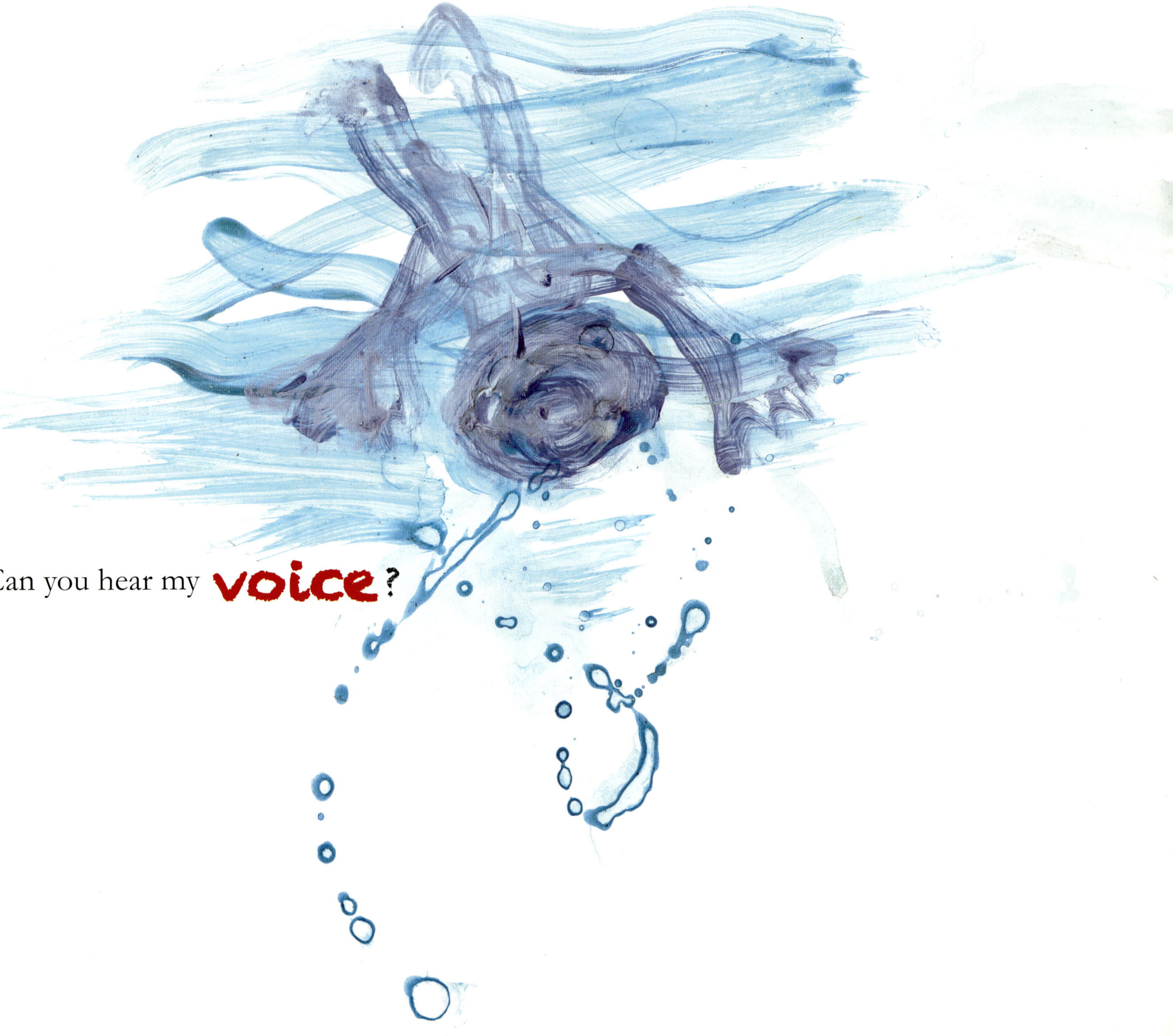

Can you hear my **voice**?

Seizo Tashima

Seizo Tashima was born in Osaka, Japan in 1940. As a graduate of Tama Art University, he has won multiple awards for his work in various picture books, such as the Biennial of Illustrations Bratislava 1969 Golden Apple Award, and 2018 Hans Christian Andersen Illustrator Award Nominee.

Picture Books for Peace from China, Korea and Japan
Boku no Koe ga Kikoemasuka (Can You Hear My Voice?)
Copyright © 2012 by Seizo Tashima

XANADU

Xanadu Publishing Ltd
25 Wharf Street, London SE8 3GG

First published in Japan in 2012 by DOSHINSHA Publishing Co., Ltd., Tokyo
English translation rights arranged with DOSHINSHA Publishing Co., Ltd.
through Japan Foreign-Rights Centre

English translation copyright © 2017 by Xanadu Publishing Ltd
ISBN 978-1-78459-136-6
A catalogue record for this book is available from the British Library.

All rights reserved. No part of this publication may be reproduced,
stored in a retrieval system,
or transmitted in any form or by any means, electronic, mechanical, photocopying,
recording or otherwise, without the prior permission of the publishers.
Printed in China
24681097531

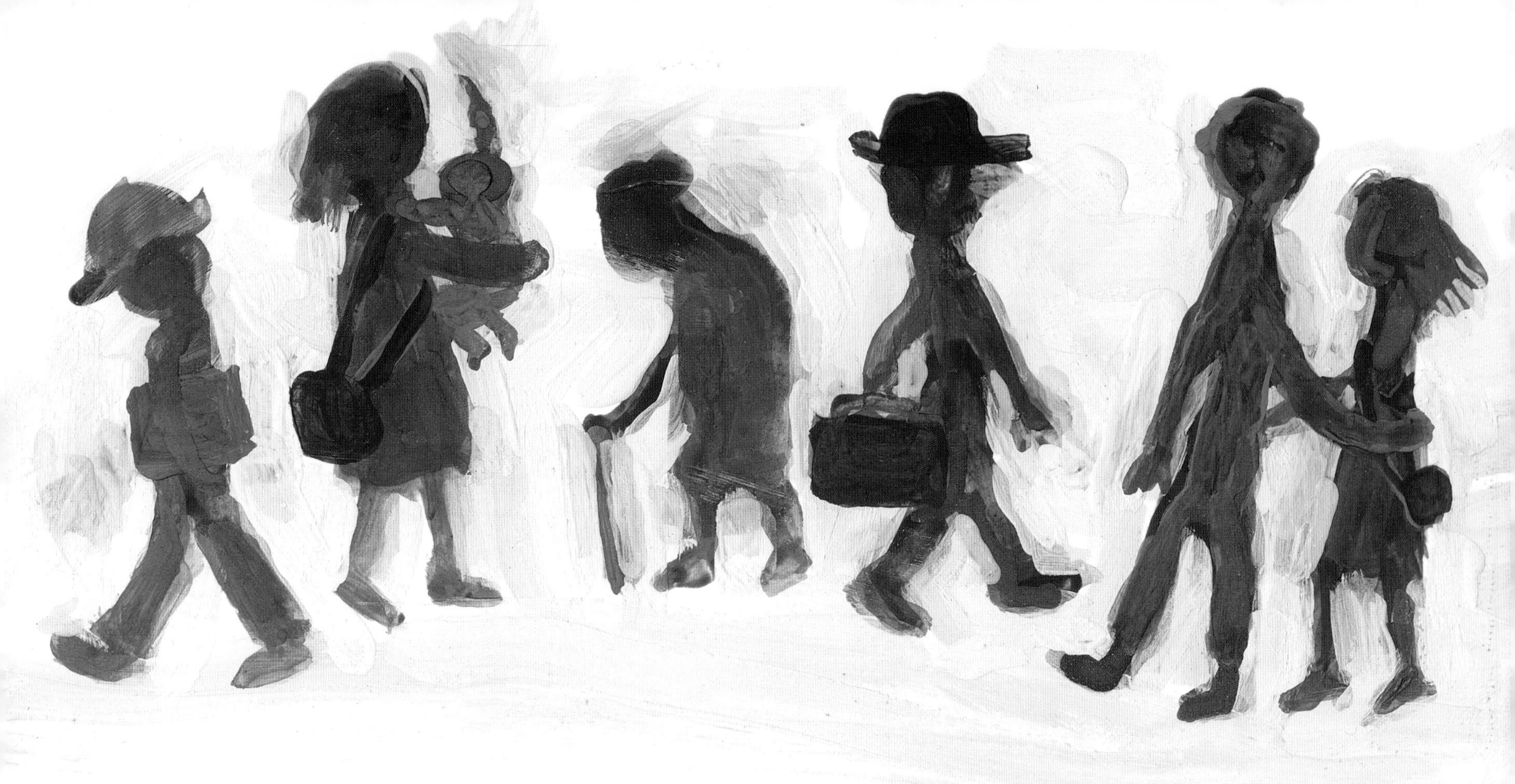